MOST High, glorious God,
enlighten the darkness of my heart
and give me true faith, certain hope, and
perfect charity,
sense and knowledge, Lord,
that I may carry out Your holy and
true command. Amen.

—St. Francis

FRANCISCAN DAILY COMPANION

MINUTE MEDITATIONS FOR EVERY DAY CONTAINING AN INSPIRATIONAL QUOTE FROM A FRANCISCAN SAINT OR BLESSED, A REFLECTION, AND A PRAYER

By
Rev. Jude Winkler, OFM Conv.

CATHOLIC BOOK PUBLISHING CORP.
New Jersey

CONTENTS

IMPRIMI POTEST: Very Rev. James McCurry, OFM Conv.
Minister Provincial of Our Lady of the Angels Province

NIHIL OBSTAT: Rev. Pawel Tomczyk, Ph.D.
Censor Librorum

IMPRIMATUR: ✠ Most Rev. Kevin A. Sweeney, D.D.
Bishop of Paterson

November 6, 2020

The Nihil Obstat and Imprimatur are official declarations that a book or a pamphlet is free of doctrinal or moral error. No implication is contained therein that those who have granted the Nihil Obstat and Imprimatur agree with the contents, opinions or statements expressed.

To the friars of Portiuncula Friary

(T-151)

ISBN 978-1-947070-83-7

Printed in China 25 HA 3

catholicbookpublishing.com

INTRODUCTION

THE origin of Franciscan Spirituality can be traced back to the founders of the Franciscan Movement: St. Francis and St. Clare. A number of the values that one can see in their lives are those that we identify as Franciscan: poverty, simplicity, obedience to the Will of God, chastity, love of the Eucharistic Lord, compassion, and many more.

But the Movement was not so fixed by its founders that it became unchangeable. Rather, toward the end of his life, St. Francis said to his followers, "I have done my part, now it is time for you to do yours."

Thus, in this meditation book on Franciscan Spirituality, we see the contributions of Franciscans of all Three Orders—from the foundation of the Movement to the present day.

Certain choices have been made in the organization of the material. Sayings have been taken from the writings and teachings of only Saints and Blesseds.

Occasionally, some of the Saints and Blesseds might not be readily recognized as Franciscan. This is true because they belonged to the Order of Secular Franciscans (e.g., Pope St. John XXIII, Bl. Veronica Antal, St. Francis de Sales, and St. John Vianney, among others).

Sayings have at times been slightly abridged in order that they might fit the space allotted. Care has been taken so that these adjustments do not change the sense of what the author intended.

The sayings have been arranged in such a way that they might reflect the tenor of the various liturgical feasts celebrated throughout the year.

May this short meditation book assist those using it to embrace the rich and profound spirituality of the Franciscan Movement.

Fr. Jude Winkler, OFM Conv.

CLING to His most sweet Mother who carried a Son Whom the heavens could not contain. —St. Clare of Assisi

JAN. 1

Mary, the Mother of God

REFLECTION. From the earliest days of the Franciscan Movement, Mary has been honored and considered to be the Mother not only of Jesus, God and Man, but also of all Franciscans.

She is the model of how Franciscans are to bear Christ to the world. She is the intercessor through whom God bestows every grace upon us.

PRAYER. *Blessed Virgin, Mother of Jesus and our Mother, pray for us.*

YOU learn to speak by speaking, to study by studying...and just so, you learn to love by loving. All those who think to learn in any other way deceive themselves. —St. Francis de Sales

JAN. 2

Great Learning

REFLECTION. While it is important to study and to learn more about the things of this world, it also is important to keep perspective. Christ is the source of all wisdom—and the goal toward which that wisdom and learning should be addressed.

Without Him, everything we learn and experience would be only meaningless facts that teach us nothing about true love.

PRAYER. *God of Wisdom, guide my mind and my heart home to You.*

JESUS, Name full of glory, grace, love and strength. —St. Bernardine of Siena

JAN. 3

The Holy Name of Jesus

REFLECTION. St. Paul wrote that everyone and everything in all of creation should bend the knee at the Name of Jesus. This Name, announced by an Angel, literally means, "Yahweh saves."

Jesus' mission and His Name were identical. All that God wanted for us—all that Jesus proclaimed to us—is that we are called to be saved in His love.

PRAYER. *Jesus, my Lord and my God; my God and my All.*

THE Lord called me to Himself with a most tender love, and with an infinite charity He led and directed me along the path of life. —Bl. Ludovico of Casoria

JAN. 4

God's Plan for Us

REFLECTION. God does not call us to follow a certain path in life just to prove that He is in charge, but rather He calls us to be the most loving people we can possibly be because He loves us.

We have to remember, however, that God sees things differently than we do—for most often, we grow to that level of love by approaching the Cross.

PRAYER. *Lord, teach me to live in Your love.*

P RIDE is the beginning of all sin; and likewise, humility is the foundation of all virtue. —St. Bonaventure

JAN. 5

O Lord, I Am Not Worthy

REFLECTION. St. Francis taught that we are what we are in the eyes of God, and nothing more. It is good to remember our smallness, our frailty, our brokenness.

It also is good, as we hear in the Letter to the Philippians, to consider others as more important than ourselves. This is not false humility, but a realistic evaluation of where we stand before God and others.

PRAYER. *Empty my heart of pride, O Lord. Teach me to follow Your example of humility.*

B E CONTENT to progress in slow steps until you have legs to run and wings with which to fly. —St. Pius of Pietrelcina

JAN. 6

Little by Little

REFLECTION. We sometimes aspire to do great things in the service of God. But He most often encounters us in the small events of everyday life—much as the Prophet Elijah met God not in the hurricane, nor the fire, nor the earthquake, but rather in the small, whispering breeze.

Small things, done with love, are great in the eyes of our God.

PRAYER. *Lord, let me not aspire to greatness, but rather to be a small one, humble in service to You.*

O MY soul, how can you refrain from plunging yourself ever deeper and deeper into the love of Christ?

—St. Angela of Foligno

JAN. 7

The Call to Be a Mystic

REFLECTION. Today we celebrate the feast day of St. Angela of Foligno, a great mystic of the Franciscan Movement.

Mysticism ultimately does not mean that one has many visions or extraordinary spiritual events. Rather, it is the ability to see the presence of the love of God in all that one sees and experiences. All of us are called to be mystics.

PRAYER. *Loving God, may my every breath, my every desire, be rooted in love of You.*

FOR the sake of a quiet conscience, despise no one.

—Bl. Giles of Assisi

JAN. 8

Love of Neighbor

REFLECTION. Inasmuch as we are called to love God with our whole being, we also are called to love our neighbor as ourselves.

Rather than hating anyone, we feel compassion for them, realizing that they are broken people who need to be healed with our love. This will bring healing both to them—and even to us—for our hearts will be at peace.

PRAYER. *Lord, teach me to love everyone whom You love.*

IN REQUESTING things, we must pray devoutly and faithfully, but not stubbornly insisting on them. —St. Anthony of Padua

JAN. 9

Trusting in God's Providence

REFLECTION. It is a good thing to ask God for those things that we need.

We wish to do this as trusting children of a loving parent and not as spoiled brats who insist on everything that they want. God, as a loving parent, often refuses to give us those things that would bring us harm.

PRAYER. *Lord, teach me to trust in Your Providence.*

OCCUPY your mind with good thoughts, or the enemy will fill them with bad ones. —St. Thomas More

JAN. 10

Thinking about the Things of the Lord

REFLECTION. In his Letter to the Philippians, St. Paul recommends that we fill our minds with things that are good and honorable and worthy of praise.

If we read good books and watch television programs and movies that are virtuous, and, if we listen to good music and enter into charitable conversations, then we will not have space in our minds and our hearts for the temptations from the evil one.

PRAYER. *May all my thoughts be charitable and honorable, Lord.*

DO NOT give yourself to others so completely that you have nothing left for yourself. —St. Charles of Borromeo

JAN. 11

Our Service to Ourselves and to Others

REFLECTION. We have to know when it is time to pull back a bit and take some time to rest, to reflect, and to recharge our batteries. If we continuously serve others without taking any time for ourselves, we end up so exhausted that we have nothing left to give.

Thus, we could even say that our taking care of ourselves is a form of service to others.

PRAYER. *Lord, grant me prudence and balance in my life.*

DO NOT walk through time without leaving worthy evidence of your passage. —Pope St. John XXIII

JAN. 12

What Is Our Heritage?

REFLECTION. The beginning of the year is a good time to ask ourselves, "What is it all about? What have I truly accomplished in the Lord? What is worthy of praise? What demands contrition? Have I given more than taken? Have I loved more than sought love?

"What will they write on my tombstone?"—or more importantly—"What impact will my life have had on others?"

PRAYER. *Lord, may my life be worthy of praise.*

EVERY evening a herald should proclaim to all the people that they are to render praise and thanks to the Lord God Almighty. —St. Francis of Assisi

JAN. 13

Praise and Gratitude

REFLECTION. We have to remember that we pray not only to obtain things for ourselves. We pray also to give something to God.

In praise, we proclaim the truth about God's greatness. In gratitude, we respond to God's goodness toward us, and we recognize our dependence upon His Providence. Our prayer should be an act of generosity and not one of selfish concern.

PRAYER. *Praise You, Lord. Thank You, Lord.*

WHAT does it matter where we go? Wherever we go, won't we be serving God there? —Bl. Solanus Casey

JAN. 14

Life Is a Pilgrimage

REFLECTION. Bl. Odoric of Pordenone was a 14th-century missionary who traveled to China to share the Faith. His life of travel and adventure reminds us that no matter where we are, no matter what we are doing, we are at home—for we are with Jesus.

His story reminds us that our faith life is a journey, and not an arrival.

PRAYER. *Lead me, Lord, in Your ways. Guide me along Your right paths.*

LET Mary never be far from your lips and from your heart. Following her, you will never lose your way.

—St. Bernardine of Siena

JAN. 15

Mary, Model of the Franciscan Life

REFLECTION. The Blessed Virgin Mary gave us an example of generous availability to the Will of God. She now intercedes on our behalf so that we, too, might respond to God's call in our lives with similar generosity.

She is the heavenly Mother who brings us consolation, but who also challenges us to be the most of what God has called us to be.

PRAYER. *Blessed Virgin Mary, teach us to be servants of the Will of God.*

LOVE that does not know of suffering is not worthy of the name. —St. Clare of Assisi

JAN. 16

The Martyrdom of Love

REFLECTION. On this commemoration of St. Berard and Companions, the first Franciscan Martyrs, we are reminded that we are called to the Cross to give witness to God's love.

We might not suffer martyrdom as St. Berard did, but we certainly will suffer what St. Thérèse of Lisieux calls white martyrdom—the annoyances of everyday life—a martyrdom of pinpricks.

PRAYER. *God, give me the courage to carry Your Cross in my everyday life.*

THERE in solitude, Francis would be able to hear God's secret revelations.
—St. Bonaventure

JAN. 17

Retreating to the Desert

REFLECTION. St. Anthony the Abbot fled the world to be alone with the Lord in a desert.

This option eludes most of us. We lead busy lives, but we still can carve out time to pull back and listen carefully to what God wants to communicate to us—for God most often speaks in whispers.

PRAYER. *Lord, may I meet You in the desert of my heart.*

SAINTS become Saints in the usual way, due to the generous fidelity to divine grace.
—St. Charles of Sezze

JAN. 18

True Sanctity

REFLECTION. How can we become Saints? We have to remember that we don't choose our path to sanctity.

It is God Who calls, God Who gives us the gifts we need to be faithful, God Who leads us in His ways. Our path is one of surrender, of collaboration with God's plan in our lives.

PRAYER. *Lead me, Lord, in the ways of Your grace.*

OBEDIENT to a carpenter! The God of eternal glory, submissive to a poor virgin! Has anyone ever heard of anything like this?

—St. Anthony of Padua

JAN. 19

Jesus, Meek and Humble

REFLECTION. Jesus fully surrendered to the Will of the Father. This action did not diminish His dignity, but rather it fulfilled the destiny to which He had been called.

Godliness lies not in acquiring power or prestige or fame. It lies in obedience to God's Will, in humility, and in meekness. Jesus teaches us these qualities by His example.

PRAYER. *Father, Your Kingdom come, Your Will be done, on earth as it is in heaven.*

HELP all without discrimination, friend and foe alike. Everyone is our neighbor.

—Bl. Angela Truszkowska

JAN. 20

We All Are Brothers and Sisters

REFLECTION. We live in a world in which people often judge each other according to their differences.

Jesus, however, especially through His parable of the Good Samaritan, has taught us that we all are sisters and brothers. We all are children of one heavenly Father, brothers and sisters of Jesus, our Savior and our Lord.

PRAYER. *Loving God, may I always remember that all are created in Your image and likeness.*

FOR those who live well in the world, death is not frightening but sweet and precious. —St. Rose of Viterbo

JAN. 21

Death as a Part of Life

REFLECTION. St. Paul, in his Letter to the Philippians, speaks of how living is good because it gives him the opportunity to serve the community; likewise, death is good because then he will be with the Lord.

One of the goals of the spiritual life is to surrender to God's Will each day until He calls us to that ultimate surrender at the moment of our death.

PRAYER. *Lord, into Your hands I commend my spirit, now, and at the hour of my death.*

HUMAN society demands that men be guided by justice, respect the rights of others and do their duty.

—Pope St. John XXIII

JAN. 22

Right to Life

REFLECTION. True justice is not that based upon human laws, but that written in our hearts by our Creator. As Pope St. John XXIII said in *Pacem in Terris*, justice must involve a profound respect for the rights of others.

Today, we must pray for—and fight for—respect for the fundamental right to life, from natural conception to natural death.

PRAYER. *God, give us the grace and courage to protect those who cannot protect themselves.*

WHAT little good we can do in this world to help and comfort the suffering, we wish to do it quietly and so far as possible unnoticed and unknown.

—St. Marianne Cope

JAN. 23

Quiet, Humble Service

REFLECTION. We do good not to be seen by others, nor to receive a reward. We serve because we want to follow Christ's example.

If no one notices, blessed are we—for it means that we can do what we do out of love and not to receive recognition or even the gratitude of those whom we serve.

PRAYER. *Lord, purify my motives so that whatever I do, I do out of love.*

DO NOT wish to be anything but what you are, and try to be that perfectly.

—St. Francis de Sales

JAN. 24

The Way to Holiness

REFLECTION. God did not ask us to be perfect in everything. Too often we measure ourselves against unrealistic expectations of what we should be.

God knows what talents and faults we have. He expects us only to do the best we can with what we are—and to do a little bit better tomorrow.

PRAYER. *Thank You, Lord, for whom You made me to be. Help me to be a little bit better than that person.*

THE mercy of God is infinitely greater than your malice.

—St. Pius of Pietrelcina

JAN. 25

The Conversion of St. Paul

REFLECTION. One of the greatest proofs that St. Paul had for the mercy of God was that he was called while he was still a sinner, a persecutor of the Church. The mercy of God is so much greater than the guilt of our sins.

While we should always be contrite for the sins we have committed, we should—even more—be grateful to God for His mercy and compassion.

PRAYER. *Compassionate Lord, have mercy on me, a sinner.*

IT IS possible to live for the next life and still be merry in this. —St. Thomas More

JAN. 26

Joy in the Spiritual Life

REFLECTION. Religious people sometimes give an impression of being dour and judgmental. But Jesus called us to be childlike in our faith, which includes having childlike joy and wonder at the many ways in which we see God's goodness in creation, in our lives, in our activities, in all things.

This, at times, even involves having the courage and mirth to be able to laugh at ourselves.

PRAYER. *Lord, may I see You in laughter, in dance, and in every way that You bring a smile to my face.*

YOU will accomplish more by kind words and a courteous manner than by anger or sharp rebuke.

—St. Angela Merici

JAN. 27

Bringing Others to Conversion

REFLECTION. Fear and guilt only bring people to conformity; only true love brings true conversion.

We see this in the way Jesus spoke to the Samaritan Woman at the well and treated her with more respect than she thought she deserved. We should treat everyone we meet with sacred respect, for they are children of God, people for whom Jesus died on the Cross.

PRAYER. *Lord, calm my anger and guard my tongue, so that I might share Your compassion in word and deed.*

MAY you infuse into us the Spirit of truth Who will teach us all truth.

—St. Bonaventure

JAN. 28

Seeking Wisdom

REFLECTION. St. Thomas Aquinas sought wisdom so that he might delve into the mysteries of our Faith.

While he was brilliant and very successful in his efforts, he nevertheless realized that he had fallen short of truly explaining the mystery—for that mystery is beyond our human ability to understand. That humility is a clear sign that he had truly learned wisdom.

PRAYER. *God, pour into my mind and heart Your Spirit of Wisdom.*

REMEMBER that the Christian life is one of action, not of speech and daydreams.

—St. Vincent Pallotti

JAN. 29

Walking the Walk

REFLECTION. It is essential that we put our values into practice in our everyday lives.

This means that we should express our faith at home, at work, on the road, in the forms of recreation we choose, in what we eat and drink; in other words, everything we do should give witness to what we believe.

PRAYER. *Lord, may what I believe truly be the basis for the way I live my life.*

CONVERSION is a grace, and grace must be entreated for with prayer.

—St. Maximilian Kolbe

JAN. 30

The Call to Conversion

REFLECTION. Flannery O'Connor speaks of how people abhor grace, because grace brings them to conversion—and conversion means that they have to change, and people hate to change.

We become so comfortable with our old ways that we fear what might await us if we were to go out into the unknown of a future filled with grace and freedom in the Spirit and God's love.

PRAYER. *Shower Your grace and love upon me, Lord, so that I might follow wherever You lead.*

WHAT we need is a cup of understanding, a barrel of love, and an ocean of patience.

—St. Francis de Sales

JAN. 31

Patience, Patience, Patience!

REFLECTION. We often are impatient with others and even with ourselves. We want everything now! But the Kingdom of God dawns in the world and in our hearts in His time, not ours.

We often have to wait for that grace-filled moment for things to come together. Patience reminds us that we are not in charge—God is.

PRAYER. *Lord, may I be as patient with others as You are with me.*

DO NOT lose heart, even if you should discover that you lack qualities necessary for the work to which you are called.

—St. Angela Merici

FEB. 1

Lacking the Needed Skills

REFLECTION. We often are cast into situations in which we are asked to perform a particular task for which we do not have the needed skills. We have to keep perspective in such situations.

If the Spirit of God called us to do something, maybe it is because we are the right person at the right time (even if we can't always see it).

PRAYER. *Lord, please supply me with what I need to do Your Will.*

NOTHING so shames and humbles the pride of a sinner than the humility of the humanity of Jesus Christ.

—St. Anthony of Padua

FEB. 2

The Presentation in the Temple

REFLECTION. Jesus, the Son of God, is brought to the Temple in Jerusalem by Mary and Joseph. Jesus, the Son of God, is a small baby. Yet, in His humility, Simeon and Anna see and recognize Him.

If we wish others to recognize that we, too, are children of God, then we must humble ourselves as Jesus did.

PRAYER. *Now Lord, You may dismiss Your servant in peace.*

GOD is the source of happiness, and whoever comes nearer to God will participate in His happiness.

—St. Maximilian Kolbe

FEB. 3

True Joy

REFLECTION. God is the source of true happiness, true joy that is unlike any that we experience in this world. The joys of this world are momentary and partial. What comes from God is eternal and complete.

That heavenly joy already begins in this world inasmuch as we live in the love of God, but it will be actualized fully in the world to come.

PRAYER. *Lord, let me live in Your joy.*

EVERY Christian must be a living book wherein one can read the teaching of the Gospel. —St. Joseph of Leonissa

FEB. 4

Becoming Living Gospels

REFLECTION. Words can be cheap. It is easy to read the Gospels, to study them, to proclaim them. It is much more difficult to live them.

Yet, this is what the world needs today: people who will commit themselves to living the Good News of salvation in their everyday lives. Like St. Francis, we have to preach not only with our words—but most of all with our lives.

PRAYER. *Lord, may I become what I have read and studied.*

A JUDICIOUS silence is always better than truth spoken without charity. —St. Francis de Sales

FEB. 5

Prudence in Our Speech

REFLECTION. Sometimes we think that we should share the absolute truth with others at all times. First of all, it might be only our version of the truth. Secondly, the other person might not be ready to hear what we have to say.

At times, it is better to hold our tongues and not say anything if that would be the more useful thing to do.

PRAYER. *Lord, teach me when to speak and when to be silent.*

AS A servant of God, do not trust yourself and your strength completely, but put all your trust in the infinite power of divine grace. —St. Vincent Pallotti

FEB. 6

Never Trust in Human Effort

REFLECTION. All throughout the Old Testament, the Prophets spoke of how we should not trust in the power of others (their horses, their arms). Likewise, we should not trust in our own efforts. (If one tries to build a house on his own, it is in vain.)

It is only possible to fulfill our divine destiny if we trust in the Lord and allow His power to work through us.

PRAYER. *You are my Strength, O Lord. You are my Rock.*

IF THERE be a true way that leads to the Everlasting Kingdom, it is most certainly that of suffering, patiently endured. —St. Colette

FEB. 7

The Gift of Suffering

REFLECTION. In the New Testament, suffering is seen not as a punishment; rather, it is an opportunity to trust in the goodness of God.

Furthermore, by offering up our suffering for the sake of someone who needs our help, we transform suffering from being something endured to something that mystically unites us with the other.

PRAYER. *Lord, I offer my suffering for N. today. May I unite my cross to Yours and to N.'s.*

IF SOMEONE speaks ill to thee, help him; if someone speaks well to thee, refer it to God.

—Bl. Giles of Assisi

FEB. 8

Nothing of My Own

REFLECTION. If someone speaks ill about you, then you should judge that action as a symptom of his or her brokenness. In that case, desire only to heal that person with your love.

If that same person speaks well of you, then it is because the Lord has granted you His blessings and the praise should be attributed to the Lord.

PRAYER. *Not to us, O Lord, but to Your Name give the glory.*

AS SOON as the soul dies to itself and becomes aware of how much it is loved, the life of grace is given to it and it lives in Christ.

—St. Angela of Foligno

FEB. 9

Transformed by Love

REFLECTION. In the Gospel of John, Jesus brings us to conversion by teaching us how much God loves us. God loves us literally to death.

The Cross is considered to be the hour of glory, for this Gospel redefines glory as the outpouring of love. Knowing that we are so greatly loved, we of course want to live in that love.

PRAYER. *Let me love You, O Jesus, Who died out of love for me.*

HOW many things are sanctified by means of God's words! By the power of Christ's words, in fact, the Sacrament of the Altar is celebrated.

—St. Francis of Assisi

FEB. 10

Word and Sacrament

REFLECTION. St. Francis had a tremendous devotion to the celebration of the Holy Mass.

During the liturgy, he was able to hear the Word of God, a Word that he felt was addressed directly to him. He was able to receive the Body and Blood of Christ, the gift of Christ's presence within his heart and soul.

PRAYER. *May my love for the celebration of the Holy Mass be as fervent as that of St. Francis.*

ONLY after the Last Judgment will Mary get any rest; from now until then, she is much too busy with her children. **—St. John Vianney**

FEB. 11

Mary, Our Intercessor

REFLECTION. The Blessed Virgin Mary does not spend her time in heaven thinking about her own needs. She is constantly interceding for her children on earth.

Mary is so loving and compassionate that she always reaches out to those in need, especially those who do not even know that what they are doing is putting them in spiritual danger.

PRAYER. *O Mary, conceived without sin, pray for us who have recourse to you.*

WITHOUT humility of heart all the other virtues by which one runs toward God seem, and are, absolutely worthless.

—St. Angela of Foligno

FEB. 12

The Fundamental Attitude

REFLECTION. Virtues are gifts that God lovingly gives us.

When humility underlies our other virtues, we recognize first of all that it is God Who makes these virtues possible in us. We should not take all the credit for them. Secondly, we realize that we have to work hard to foster these virtues; otherwise, they will wither and die.

PRAYER. *Humble my heart, O Lord, so that I always acknowledge You as the source of all good things.*

[**J**ESUS,] Whose graciousness is our joy, Whose gentleness fills us to overflowing, Whose remembrance brings a gentle light.

—St. Clare of Assisi

FEB. 13

Jesus, Whose Goodness Overwhelms Us

REFLECTION. As St. Clare contemplated upon the goodness and kindness of God, she was filled to overflowing with joy and gratitude. She experienced Him not as a stern judge, but rather as a gentle love.

The more we know that love in our own lives, the more we want to reject anything that would separate us from it.

PRAYER. *Gracious and gentle Lord, fill me with Your love.*

FRIENDSHIP demands attention.

—St. Thomas More

FEB. 14

Becoming a Friend of God

REFLECTION. We can learn a lot about our relationship with God by considering our human relationships. God loves us with a father's and a mother's love. Jesus is our brother—but God also should be our friend.

Jesus said that we are not servants but His friends. What in our relationship with our friends could be applied to our relationship with God?

PRAYER. *Lord, may I always work at my friendship with You.*

GOD commands you to pray, but forbids you to worry. —St. John Vianney

FEB. 15

Trusting in God

REFLECTION. It can be difficult at times to trust in God's Providence, especially when things are not going our way. Prayer, by definition, is an act of trust, and it can calm us when we are filled with anxiety.

Even if our prayer is one of frustration and anger, the very fact that we are still speaking to God in prayer means that we trust that He is listening.

PRAYER. *Calm my anxious heart, O Lord.*

CHARITY is the soul of faith, makes it alive; without love, faith dies.

—St. Anthony of Padua

FEB. 16

Faith and Works

REFLECTION. Faith is not simply an intellectual activity. It is not only an acceptance of certain dogmas proclaimed by the Church. Rather, it is an act of profound trust in the promises made by God that were fulfilled by Jesus.

Faith, therefore, cannot be passive. It must be witnessed by works of charity that incarnate our beliefs.

PRAYER. *May I give witness to my faith by my works of charity done in Your Name.*

WHENEVER I see a wall between Christians, I try to pull out a brick.

—Pope St. John XXIII

FEB. 17

Healing the Rifts

REFLECTION. There are too many divisions in our fractured world for us to create new ones. We have to find a way to heal these wounds, especially among those who follow the teaching of Christ.

We are not true disciples of the Prince of Peace when we attack other Christians and berate them. We have to treat them with respect, even learning from some of their ideas and practices.

PRAYER. *Lord, make us one flock, with You as our one Shepherd.*

W ITH swift pace, light step, and unswerving feet, go forward securely, joyfully and swiftly on the path of prudent happiness.

—St. Clare of Assisi

FEB. 18

Following the Path of the Lord

REFLECTION. St. Clare's words remind us how we should follow the path of the Lord with joy and confidence. While all of us occasionally have doubts, we have to put them out of our minds and be trusting. We cannot let those doubts shake our confidence.

Consider an old saying when in doubt: we can wonder if we are on the right bus—just don't get off.

PRAYER. *Direct my feet, O Lord, along Your path.*

W HEN St. Francis went for alms, he was moved by a liberty of spirit and not by greed.

—St. Bonaventure

FEB. 19

Seeking What We Need

REFLECTION. St. Francis had no problem asking for assistance from others when his own work could not satisfy his needs, but he did not want to accumulate possessions.

He did not judge his task as successful if he had collected large amounts of food, but rather if he had enough for himself and to share with those who had less.

PRAYER. *Lord, when I seek help from others, may it not be to add to my riches.*

IF YOU would find grace, be discerning, reverent, amiable, frank and sweet.

—Bl. Giles of Assisi

FEB. 20

Seeking God's Grace

REFLECTION. It is a very good thing to seek to live in God's grace, but we must do so with a gentleness of manner that does not contradict the very thing we seek.

Some people who try to be spiritual also become judgmental and angry and arrogant in the way they treat people who do not meet their standards.

PRAYER. *May I truly live, O Lord, what I seek.*

HALF an hour's meditation each day is essential, except when you are busy. Then a full hour is needed.

—St. Francis de Sales

FEB. 21

Our Daily Meditation

REFLECTION. There is so much to do these days that taking time out for meditation can sometimes seem to be a selfish luxury, but it actually is essential.

Otherwise, we will lose perspective and begin to react to situations without thinking or praying. Even other faiths and nonreligious people recognize the value of meditation.

PRAYER. *Lord, lead me to a quiet place to be with You alone.*

HIS only anxiety of mind now was to discover how he might conform perfectly to the rule given to the Apostles.
—St. Bonaventure

FEB. 22

The Chair of Peter

REFLECTION. St. Francis wanted to follow in the footsteps of Christ and the Apostles. For this reason, he always was faithful and respectful to the successors of those Apostles—the prelates of the Church—and especially to the successor of St. Peter, the Holy Father.

He understood that obedience to God began with obedience to the one appointed to lead His Church.

PRAYER. *St. Peter the Apostle, pray for us.*

SAINTS have found their paradise here on earth in poverty, humiliations and suffering, which they accepted for the love of God.
—St. Maximilian Kolbe

FEB. 23

Suffering with Christ

REFLECTION. When we speak of heaven on earth, we often mean that things are going well, that we have been successful, and that we are enjoying life.

But St. Maximilian Kolbe reminds us that heaven on earth is actually measured by how greatly we love, and it is often in difficulties that the true measure of our love is determined.

PRAYER. *May I always view my times of suffering not as a curse, but rather as a blessing.*

MAY our heart be gentle, Christ-like, towards the wretched and those who suffer. —Bl. Jacques Ghazir Haddad

FEB. 24

Our Service of the Poor

REFLECTION. Each of us is called to practice the corporal works of mercy toward those who need our love and our care.

Like St. Francis with the lepers, like St. Teresa of Calcutta with the destitute and dying, we must try to see the face of the suffering Christ in all those whom we serve.

PRAYER. *Lord, grant that I seek not to be served, but rather to serve.*

BY PRACTICING the most perfect interior and exterior purity, he did everything he could to preserve it as something holy and held in honor. —St. Bonaventure

FEB. 25

Pure of Heart and Pure of Body

REFLECTION. In the Letter to the Romans, St. Paul speaks of consecrating our bodies to the service of the Lord.

God created our bodies and they are good—but because of our fallen nature, we can very easily let our passions control us and misuse this gift from God. Like St. Francis, we must seek to live truly chaste lives.

PRAYER. *Preserve me, O Lord, from all that would cause me to treat my body in an undignified manner.*

THE Holy Eucharist is a fire that purifies and consumes all our miseries and imperfections. —St. Hyacinth of Mariscotti

FEB. 26

Our God Is a Consuming Fire

REFLECTION. The image of fire is often used in spiritual literature. Fire can purify what is impure. Fire produces heat and light. Our love provides heat in a world filled with cold indifference. Light guides us through the darkness of confusion and doubt.

The Holy Eucharist, the very love of God Incarnate, is a spiritual fire that purifies, warms, and guides.

PRAYER. *May my heart burn with the fire of Your love, O Lord.*

ACTIONS speak louder than words; let your words teach and your actions speak. —St. Anthony of Padua

FEB. 27

Teaching and Living

REFLECTION. It is important to give witness to our faith in words. Especially nowadays we have to be ready to explain why we believe what we do.

But those words would be empty if we did not give witness to them by the way we live our lives. Yes, we should teach others, but we can do so only by both our words and actions.

PRAYER. *I believe, O Lord, and so I will act.*

MOST High, Glorious God, enlighten the darkness of my heart.

—St. Francis of Assisi

FEB. 28

Prayer before the Crucifix

REFLECTION. This quote is the beginning of St. Francis' Prayer before the Crucifix. He realized that it was the Cross that would bring enlightenment to his heart.

The Cross is the ultimate lesson on love. It teaches us how we should live in rapport with God (surrender to His Will) and with the world (willing to die out of love for our neighbor).

PRAYER. *Lord, give me right faith, fervent hope, and perfect charity.*

ACT today in such a way that you need not blush tomorrow. —St. John Bosco

FEB. 29

Do the Right Thing

REFLECTION. At times, spiritual wisdom is not a series of deep, profound truths. Sometimes it is the most practical and common-sense things.

If we do the right thing, then there will be nothing that will embarrass us in the future. If we do not—even if others don't know what we have done—there will be turmoil in our hearts that will rob us of our peace.

PRAYER. *May everything I do today be virtuous, worthy of praise.*

[J]ESUS,] Whose beauty all the heavenly hosts admire unceasingly, Whose love inflames our love, Whose contemplation is our refreshment.

—St. Clare of Assisi

MAR. 1

Jesus, All Beautiful

REFLECTION. The beauty of Our Lord Jesus Christ is not based upon physical beauty. It is that inner beauty of a person who is fully committed to love of God and love of neighbor.

Seeing that beauty refreshes our spirits in a world often filled with the ugliness of selfishness and greed. This is the beauty to which we aspire.

PRAYER. *Lord Jesus, may I look upon Your beauty and seek it for myself.*

HOLD fast what you have. Keep on doing what you are doing. Do not depart from your course. —St. Agnes of Prague

MAR. 2

Persistence

REFLECTION. It is not easy to do the same thing day after day. This is why we pray for perseverance.

The habit that we form by doing the right thing, by finding the enthusiasm to do the same old thing again and again—each time as if it were the first and only time we were doing it—gives witness to the true intentions of our hearts.

PRAYER. *Loving God, may I always be consistent in my commitment to Your Kingdom.*

HOLY contrition, holy humility, holy charity, holy devotion and holy joy make the soul holy and good.

—Bl. Giles of Assisi

MAR. 3

Conversion of Our Hearts and Our Actions

REFLECTION. True conversion requires a purification of the motives of our hearts. This involves a spirit of contrition for our wrongs and the humility to see ourselves as God sees us.

Also, we must express our conversion by showing charity to those who need our love and joy, which are so important in a world filled with negativity and gloom.

PRAYER. *Lord, make me one with You, inside and out.*

THOSE who are called to the table of the Lord must glow with the brightness that comes from the good example of a praiseworthy and blameless life.

—St. John of Capistrano

MAR. 4

The Eucharist Leading Us to Holiness

REFLECTION. While we do not have to be perfect to receive the Eucharist, we should be perfected when we receive it. The love we receive in the Eucharist should lead us to an ever more profound conversion.

It is a terrible scandal for people to see us receiving the Eucharist and then leaving church and acting in a way that is inconsistent with our Christian calling.

PRAYER. *Lord, may I become what I receive.*

THERE was never an angry man who thought that his anger was unjust.

—St. Francis de Sales

MAR. 5

Why Am I So Angry?

REFLECTION. Very strong emotions can provide the opportunity to ask ourselves why what is happening is so disturbing to us.

Is it because it reminds us of a past hurt? Does it threaten something that we want to preserve? Does what is being said or done actually reveal a truth that we would prefer to stay hidden?

PRAYER. *Lord, preserve me from an unjust and futile anger.*

THE fruitfulness of work does not depend on abilities, efforts or money.... It only and exclusively depends on our degree of union with God.

—St. Maximilian Kolbe

MAR. 6

To Do Everything in the Lord

REFLECTION. We tend to measure our success in terms of what others say of us, or how much money we make, or how successfully we accomplish our tasks.

But the true measure of the value of our work is how much this work was done with love—and how much it was done in the Lord.

PRAYER. *May all I do, O Lord, be done in and through You.*

WE BELONG not to ourselves but to Him who redeemed us.
—St. Braulio of Saragossa

MAR. 7

I Am Not My Own

REFLECTION. It is essential to remember that we were created not for a life filled with selfishness, but rather to live in the salvation that God offers us.

That salvation necessarily entails embracing God's plan for us, which is that we live as Jesus did: in service, and generosity, and compassion. We also have to make God the center of all we are and do.

PRAYER. *Let me always remember why I was created and what You desire that I be and do.*

THE created world is itself a ladder leading us up toward God. —St. Bonaventure

MAR. 8

Creation Leading Us to God

REFLECTION. If we reflect upon the beauty and wonder of creation, we naturally will be led to a spirit of admiration and gratitude toward the Creator.

Our dominion over creation is not the ability to exploit it for our own purposes, but rather treating it as we see in Psalm 8: celebrating it with a childlike sense of awe.

PRAYER. *Lord, may I see in everything the fingerprints of Your work.*

HOPE everything from the mercy of God; it is as boundless as His power.

—St. Frances of Rome

MAR. 9

God Who Is All Merciful

REFLECTION. The mercy that we see on the Cross is not a case of God changing His mind about us. The Cross is actually the sacrament, the outward sign of an invisible reality—the mercy of God.

The problem of our sin is not God's; it is ours. Sin is turning our backs on the mercy that God is always offering us.

PRAYER. *God, have mercy on me, a sinner.*

MODERATE yourself in food and drink because they war against the soul.

—Bl. Giles of Assisi

MAR. 10

Discipline in the Spiritual Life

REFLECTION. While food and drink are gifts from God, they can be misused because of our fallen nature. We can eat or drink too much—or the wrong thing.

We have to practice a spiritual discipline to make sure that we use the gifts of God in the right way. Love often means saying, "No" when it is appropriate.

PRAYER. *May even my eating and drinking give praise to You, O Lord.*

MY LIFE'S desire was, and is today to do missionary work.

—Bl. Miguel Tomaszek

MAR. 11

The Feast of Bl. Agnellus of Pisa

REFLECTION. Bl. Agnellus was a missionary of the Franciscan Charism. He founded the Franciscan presence in England during the lifetime of St. Francis of Assisi.

The friars quickly founded their fraternity in Canterbury (religious capital), in London (political capital), and in Oxford (academic capital). This is a reminder that the Franciscan calling should be involved in every aspect of our lives.

PRAYER. *Bl. Agnellus of Pisa, pray for us.*

OUR condition is most noble, being so beloved of the Most High God that He was willing to die for our sake.

—St. Angela of Foligno

MAR. 12

Oh, How Much God Loves Us!

REFLECTION. We have to remember the great dignity to which God has called us. God chose us to experience His salvation from before the foundation of the world. Our names were written in the Book of Life before we were born.

God always intended us to share in His life and His love. We only have to give our assent.

PRAYER. *Lord, each day may I become more of what You intended me to be.*

DO NOT ask for anything unless God has moved you to ask.

—St. Paschal Baylon

MAR. 13

The Spirit Teaches Us How We Should Pray

REFLECTION. Our minds and hearts can become so focused on the things of this world that we do not even know for what we should pray.

It is the Spirit Who instructs us concerning what we truly need. It is then the Spirit Who teaches us how to pray. On our own, we could easily seek transitory things that do not bring true consolation.

PRAYER. *Lord, teach me how to pray and for what I should pray.*

RUN, jump, shout, but do not sin.

—St. John Bosco

MAR. 14

Do Anything but Sin

REFLECTION. Being a Christian does not mean living a life filled with gloom and guilt. We can be involved in many things in this world: family life, sports, art, recreation, community, etc.

We can partake of these interests in a godly way. Rather than running away from the things of the world, we can consecrate them in God's love.

PRAYER. *Lord, teach me to make each moment and each activity a proclamation of Your Kingdom.*

JESUS warns us not to be sad in doing penance, so that penance may arise from love. —St. Maximilian Kolbe

MAR. 15

Brothers and Sisters of Penance

REFLECTION. St. Francis considered Franciscans to be brothers and sisters of penance. But penance is not a gloomy rejection of anything that is fun. It is a conversion of our hearts so that we can embrace the only thing that truly matters in life: Christ.

We should see our penitential practices as acts of love that fill us with joy.

PRAYER. *May my penance free my soul from its egoism.*

IT IS impossible for the devil to enter where love abides. —Bl. Giles of Assisi

MAR. 16

Love Defeats the Evil One

REFLECTION. When Jesus died on the Cross, the devil thought he had won. But love always conquers evil.

Consider our lives. If we fill them with love and generosity of spirit, then the devil does not have the slightest chance of corrupting our hearts. But we must continually examine our conscience to make sure that what we call love is truly godly.

PRAYER. *Lord, teach me to love as You love.*

BLESSED the religious who is always willing to be corrected. —St. Francis of Assisi

MAR. 17

We Are Not Always Right

REFLECTION. We easily can become defensive when others try to correct us. It is possible that what they are saying is wrong, or it could be partially right.

Despite what people say, we should be able to accept correction humbly. We can consider what they have pointed out during our examination of conscience.

PRAYER. *May I humbly accept correction, O Lord, and learn from what others say to me.*

OUR flesh is not bronze, nor is our strength that of stone, rather we are frail, and inclined to every bodily weakness! —St. Clare of Assisi

MAR. 18

Our Fragility

REFLECTION. It is a good thing to recognize our own fragility. Our bodily strength is limited, our intellectual ability has its bounds—even our faith is subject to doubts and confusion.

Yet, God supplies what we cannot. Furthermore, our limitations mean that we have to seek God's assistance, as well as that of those around us—which is a good practice.

PRAYER. *Lord, in my weakness, I ask You to be my strength.*

THE deeper the roots of humility are imbedded in the heart, the higher will rise the edifice of good works.

—St. Anthony of Padua

MAR. 19

To Be as Humble as St. Joseph

REFLECTION. We hear no brilliant discourses from St. Joseph in the Gospels, nor is he seen to perform any great miracles. But in his humble, constant service, he gave us an example of how we can respond to God's call.

We should not call attention to ourselves. We should not seek gratitude from others. We simply should do what God calls us to do.

PRAYER. *St. Joseph, spouse of the Blessed Virgin Mary, pray for us.*

WHEN you are at Mass, be there as if you were on Calvary.

—Bl. John of Parma

MAR. 20

Passing outside of Time

REFLECTION. In the celebration of the Sacrament of the Eucharist, we pass outside of time. In those moments, we enter eternity: we are present at the Last Supper, under the Cross, and at the Resurrection.

Being on Calvary, we see with our own eyes the love with which God has always loved us.

PRAYER. *O Holy Banquet, in which the memory of the Passion is recalled, be my sustenance.*

MAN'S greatness lies in being faithful to the present moment.

—Bl. Solanus Casey

MAR. 21

Encountering God in the Present

REFLECTION. We easily can become so concerned about past memories or fear what will happen in the future that we lose track of the fact that God is acting in our present.

It is good to slow down and meditate each day on how we have met God and how we have embraced His saving plan for us.

PRAYER. *Open my eyes and my heart, O Lord, to recognize Your presence.*

THERE is no better means of attainment to the spiritual life than by continually beginning again. —St. Francis de Sales

MAR. 22

Over and Over Again

REFLECTION. We sometimes become frustrated by the fact that we don't seem to be able to change a bad behavior, even though we have tried over and over again.

It is Satan who wants us to become discouraged so we stop trying. The challenge is to keep trying, because one of these days our efforts will succeed.

PRAYER. *Lord, I thank You that You are willing to forgive me seventy times seven.*

ANY time spent before the Eucharistic presence, be it long or short, is the best spent time of our lives.

—St. Catherine of Genoa

MAR. 23

Eucharistic Adoration

REFLECTION. Our celebration of the Mass emphasizes the communal dimension of our faith. But we all need some quiet time before our Eucharistic Lord so that we can encounter Him one on one.

What an incredible gift in this noisy and busy world—to be able to spend some quiet time with the One Whom we most love.

PRAYER. *Jesus, like St. Thomas, I call upon You as my Lord and my God.*

IT IS my heart's ardent yearning to belong entirely to God and to do His Will, not to depart one iota from what God wants from me.

—Bl. Didacus Joseph of Cadiz

MAR. 24

Embracing God's Plan for Us

REFLECTION. Our hearts can be so complicated, with so many motives for the things we do—which often are hidden even from ourselves.

We ask God to purify our minds and hearts so that we might embrace His Will without reserve. The more that we do this, the more we become who we were created to be.

PRAYER. *Your Kingdom come, Your Will be done, on earth, as it is in heaven.*

YOU who surpass our understanding have become understandable. You who are uncreated have become a creature.
—St. Angela of Foligno

MAR. 25

The Annunciation

REFLECTION. How could the Son of God, through Whom all things were created, become Incarnate? How could the eternal Only Begotten Son of the Father enter time? How could He Who is all powerful, all knowing, and omnipresent assume the limitations of the human condition?

None of this makes any sense, but it is true.

PRAYER. *Let it be done unto me according to Your Word.*

YOU must befriend one another, as Christ has befriended you, to the honor of God. —St. Anthony of Padua

MAR. 26

Friend of God, Friend of Neighbor

REFLECTION. Our faith has a vertical dimension: our relationship with God, but it also has a horizontal dimension: the relationships we have with those around us.

A holy friendship in which there is mutual generosity and support can lead us to desire that greater friendship with the Lord. And our friendship with the Lord gives us the grace to form true friendships.

PRAYER. *Lord, grant that I might be a good friend to You and to those around me.*

EVERY creature in heaven and on earth and in the depths of the sea should give God praise and glory and honor and blessing.

—St. Francis of Assisi

MAR. 27

Praise and Glory to God

REFLECTION. St. Francis recognized that the created world is not opposed to the goodness of God, but rather it is a manifestation of that goodness.

And creation praises God simply by doing those things for which it was created to do. This is why St. Francis wrote *The Canticle of the Creatures* and why he would call upon nature (e.g., the birds of the sky) to praise God.

PRAYER. *Be You praised, my Lord, for and by all of Your creation.*

HOWEVER well-developed human reason may be it is a blind guide for man's mind to follow in his attempts to understand the secrets of heaven.

—St. Bernardine of Siena

MAR. 28

The Mysteries of Our Faith

REFLECTION. There is so much about our Faith that we cannot know through analysis. The ways of God are far beyond our comprehension. The ways of God are mysterious. We should not expect to figure it all out.

Faith is not necessarily a question of understanding as much as believing—trusting what often cannot be explained.

PRAYER. *Lord, teach me to believe even what I cannot understand.*

WE ARE made loveless by our possessions. —St. Elizabeth of Hungary

MAR. 29

Love and Poverty

REFLECTION. St. Elizabeth of Hungary, who as queen was quite rich, surrendered everything to serve the poor. She realized that in trying to hold on to things, we become imprisoned by what we possess.

It is only in poverty that we stop holding on to what we have in order to share it with others.

PRAYER. *Lord, teach me true and holy poverty.*

IF YOU find it impossible to pray, hide behind your good Angel and charge him to pray in your stead. —St. John Vianney

MAR. 30

When We Cannot Pray

REFLECTION. There are times when we feel that we cannot pray. It might be because we are angry or depressed because we are experiencing a great difficulty. It might be because we feel distracted. It might even be because we simply feel dry, as if we have nothing left to give.

Whatever the cause, we can call upon the Saints and Angels to pray with and for us.

PRAYER. *I thank and praise, You, O Lord, for Your Saints and Angels.*

GOD, who loves tiny beginnings, will know as He always does know, how and when to provide developments.

—Bl. Solanus Casey

MAR. 31

In God's Time

REFLECTION. We often want things done in our time. We have plans, programs, procedures. Yet, most spiritual developments are done in God's time and not ours.

The Bible has two words for time: *chronos* (which means one minute after the other) and *kairos* (which means the appointed time, God's time). Salvation occurs in *kairos*.

PRAYER. *Lord, teach me to give all my effort, but to remember that all will happen in Your time.*

WE IN the beginning of our vocation were fervent in doing fruitful and bitter penance, but after a time we became cold and lukewarm.

—Bl. Giles of Assisi

APR. 1

Persistence

REFLECTION. Most of us experience an initial enthusiasm when we first come to the Lord. This is true especially if our conversion is significant (e.g., from another religion). The difficulty is that after a while, the enthusiasm wears off and we begin to compromise on our commitment.

Every day, we have to renew our fervor for doing what is right.

PRAYER. *Renew my spirit, O Lord, so that I might serve You with zeal.*

IF THROUGH human weakness we fail, we must always without delay arise again by means of holy penance. —St. Colette

APR. 2

Seeking Forgiveness

REFLECTION. God is always ready to forgive us our sins. The problem with sin is never God, but rather us turning our backs on God's love.

When we go to the Sacrament of Reconciliation, admit our sinfulness, and ask for forgiveness, we hear the words of the priest that our sins are truly and fully forgiven.

PRAYER. *Forgive me, O Lord, for I have sinned.*

INTO whatever house the friars enter, let them first say, "Peace to this house!" —St. Francis of Assisi

APR. 3

Bring Peace to the World

REFLECTION. In the Letter to the Philippians, St. Paul writes of how two members of the community were feuding. He asks the community to help them to make peace.

Our duty is not to take one side or another; nor is it to try to make the problem worse. The Lord calls us to bring His peace to all whom we meet.

PRAYER. *May Your peace reign upon the earth.*

HOLINESS consists not in extraordinary deeds, but in performing your duties toward God, toward yourself and toward others well. —St. Maximilian Kolbe

APR. 4

Small Things with Great Love

REFLECTION. We sometimes wonder why God does not reveal Himself to us in a powerful way. We forget that He already is revealing Himself in many small ways daily throughout our lives.

Small things done with great love give a powerful witness to our faith. They also remind those who see us that God is still very present in our world.

PRAYER. *May I always find You in the small, humble events of everyday life.*

YOU must speak to Jesus not only with your lips, but with your heart.

—St. Pius of Pietrelcina

APR. 5

Heartfelt Prayer

REFLECTION. There is always a danger when we pray of going through the motions without reflecting upon what we are doing. This is true especially in prayers like the Rosary and Christian Prayer, for the words are provided for us.

Before we pray and while we are praying, we have to remind ourselves what we are doing and why.

PRAYER. *May my prayers not be empty words, but rather the deepest expressions of my heart.*

THOSE who are truly sorry for their sins do not seek excuses to make their sins seem less than they are.

—St. Anthony of Padua

APR. 6

Admitting Our Sinfulness

REFLECTION. Many of us become experts at rationalizing our actions or blaming the consequences of our choices on others (even on the devil).

If we truly want to experience the pardon of the Lord, we have to admit our sinfulness to its full degree—and we have to seek His pardon and mercy. Otherwise, we simply will be playing a game, presuming upon God's goodness.

PRAYER. *Lord, I truly am a sinner; forgive my sins.*

GOD has always protected you, and loves you as a mother.

—St. Clare of Assisi

APR. 7

As a Mother Loves Her Child, Even More Does God Love Us

REFLECTION. In the Book of the Prophet Isaiah, we hear that even if a mother were to forget her child, God would never forget us.

God loves us with a father's love and a mother's love. A father's love calls for fidelity to the Commandments; a mother's love calls for compassion to those who have fallen short.

PRAYER. *God, thank You for loving me with a father's and a mother's love.*

FREE from every stain, St. Francis' genius pierced to the heart of its mysteries.

—St. Bonaventure

APR. 8

A Childlike Wonder

REFLECTION. It often is not the highly educated person who can delve into the mysteries of God, but those who live in simplicity. They don't feel the need to understand and articulate everything. They simply can be open to and accept what goes beyond their understanding.

St. Francis, having purified his heart of vice, was able to be childlike in his approach to God.

PRAYER. *Lord, may I purify my heart to become truly simple.*

BE CONFIDENT in making your needs known to one another.

—St. Francis of Assisi

APR. 9

We Need Each Other

REFLECTION. We often do not want to bother others with our problems. We feel that they already have enough concerns. Besides, we prefer to do things on our own.

But not asking others for help when we truly need it is not only being arrogantly self-sufficient, it also is robbing from them the opportunity to show their love by serving us.

PRAYER. *May I never be afraid to ask for help from You or from my neighbor.*

OUR perfection certainly consists in knowing God and ourselves.

—St. Angela of Foligno

APR. 10

Know Thyself, Know God

REFLECTION. One of the tasks in the spiritual life is truly to know oneself. The human heart hides levels of motivations that can influence our thoughts and actions. We must come to know them.

As we come to know ourselves, we become more free to come to know better Who God is and what He wants of us. Then, the more we know God, the more we can know ourselves.

PRAYER. *Lord, send me Your Wisdom and Knowledge.*

IT IS impossible for man to ascend to the grace of God or to persevere in it without holy fear and holy dread. —Bl. Giles of Assisi

APR. 11

Fear of the Lord

REFLECTION. Fear of the Lord does not mean to be afraid of God. The First Letter of St. John clearly says that where there is love, there is no fear. Fear of the Lord is recognition of His holiness and greatness.

We are simple, humble creatures, while God is so wondrous. This proper perspective leads us to surrender to His Will.

PRAYER. *Great and glorious are You, O Lord.*

GIVE me correct faith, sure hope and perfect charity, with understanding and knowledge. —St. Francis of Assisi

APR. 12

The Theological Virtues

REFLECTION. We are called to live a virtuous life, and that requires constant spiritual work. But we have to remember that the virtues are first of all gifts from the Lord, and the ability to respond to those virtues is also a gift.

That does not negate our responsibility, but it does put in perspective the fact that God is the source of all good gifts.

PRAYER. *Lord, grant me the ability to live a life of virtue.*

LORD, give me a sense of humor so that I may take some happiness from this life and share it with others. —St. Thomas More

APR. 13

Laughter as a Form of Prayer

REFLECTION. St. Francis taught us how to be childlike in our appreciation of all that God provides for us, and especially in creation. Sometimes we become too solemn in our faith.

Like St. Francis, every once in a while we have to pick up two sticks and pretend we are playing the violin. We have to laugh and play and celebrate the goodness of God.

PRAYER. *Lord, let me never forget to smile!*

GOD created us through His kindness, grace and love; therefore we by nature ought to be kind and full of grace.

—Bl. Giles of Assisi

APR. 14

Being Gentle in the World

REFLECTION. God created us because He wanted to share the love of the Trinity with others. We were created out of love and for love.

God showed compassion to us when we turned from Him in sin. We should be willing to treat others with the same love and compassion that we have received from God.

PRAYER. *Let my every action toward others be filled with Your love and compassion.*

THE devil runs away when we make the Sign of the Cross. —St. Anthony of Padua

APR. 15

The Power of the Cross

REFLECTION. On the Cross, evil was defeated by love; death was defeated by life eternal.

When we remember the Cross of Christ, Satan realizes that he cannot entice or control us because we have chosen to associate with God's love. When we carry our own crosses to be one with Christ, Satan is defeated.

PRAYER. *May I embrace Your Cross, O Lord, so that the crosses of my life will be one with Yours.*

AMONG all the devotions approved by the Church, none has been favored by so many miracles as the devotion of the Most Holy Rosary. —Pope St. Pius X

APR. 16

Praying the Rosary

REFLECTION. The commemoration of St. Bernadette reminds us that we are called to foster a real and profound devotion to the Blessed Virgin Mary.

Over the centuries, the Rosary has been a privileged form of devotion. As we pray the Rosary, we unite with those praying it around the world, and even with those who prayed it throughout the ages.

PRAYER. *Mary, Queen of the Most Holy Rosary, pray for us.*

WHEN a man is too sure of himself, he becomes less wary of the enemy. —St. Bonaventure

APR. 17

Pride Goes before the Fall

REFLECTION. In the Book of Revelation, the members of the Church of Laodicea are told that God would prefer them either hot or cold. Hot means on fire with love for the Lord. Cold means that if they were to be sinners, it was better to be big sinners.

The real danger lies in complacency, that is, thinking that all the calls to conversion are addressed to someone else.

PRAYER. *May I not concentrate on what I have accomplished, but rather on what I still have to do.*

APR. 18

ANYONE who clings to his own opinions in the depths of his heart has not renounced the world perfectly.

—St. Francis of Assisi

True Poverty of Heart

REFLECTION. It is much easier to renounce physical possessions than it is to renounce those attitudes that we hold in our hearts. There often are opinions, prejudices, and set ideas that can control our conduct.

True poverty means that we are willing to plumb our thoughts and convictions and call them into question in the light of the Gospel.

PRAYER. *Lord, may my thoughts and attitudes belong to You alone.*

APR. 19

NOTHING is so strong as gentleness, nothing so gentle as real strength.

—St. Frances of Rome

Blessed Are the Meek

REFLECTION. When we are faced with injustice and wrong conduct, the temptation is to resort to aggressive behavior to fight the evil. Ironically, in so doing, we are adopting Satan's techniques and are betraying the very thing we claim to be protecting.

The only true way to defeat evil is with love and humility and gentleness. The power of evil cannot overcome these virtues.

PRAYER. *Lord, calm my spirit and teach me to be meek.*

GO FORTH without fear, for He Who created you has made you holy.

—St. Clare of Assisi

APR. 20

God Does What We Cannot Do on Our Own

REFLECTION. When we consider the many ways that we have fallen away from God's grace, we easily can become discouraged. Furthermore, there are those sins and bad habits that never seem to go away—and we are tempted to give up trying.

But God can heal our brokenness and give us the strength to do great and holy things.

PRAYER. *Transform me, O Lord, in Your Holiness.*

MY BOOK is the crucifix. I have only to raise my eyes to that to learn gentleness and humility.

—St. Conrad of Parzham

APR. 21

The School of the Cross

REFLECTION. The Letter to the Philippians speaks of how Jesus humbled Himself, even to dying on the Cross.

His humility and His refusal to respond to violence with violence—accepting His Passion with the meekness of a lamb—is a tremendous lesson for each of us as we try to confront difficult situations and difficult people.

PRAYER. *Most High Glorious God, enlighten the darkness of my heart.*

ST. FRANCIS made all creation a ladder by which he might mount up and embrace Him Who is all desirable. —St. Bonaventure

APR. 22

The Fingerprints of God

REFLECTION. St. Francis of Assisi saw creation as a special gift from God, and even more, as his brother and sister. He treated it with sacred respect, even proclaiming the Word of God to the birds of the air and protecting animals like lambs and even worms.

On this Earth Day, we are reminded of our responsibility to safeguard the integrity of creation.

PRAYER. *Be You praised, my Lord, with all Your creatures.*

TO CONTEMPLATE is to be separated from all and to be united to God alone. —Bl. Giles of Assisi

APR. 23

The Call to Contemplation

REFLECTION. While yesterday we celebrated the fact that we can see the fingerprints of God in all of creation, today we remember that we also are called to contemplate God Himself.

This requires a bit of separation from everyday things. We have to find silence and solitude, if only for a brief interlude, to allow us to be one with Him alone.

PRAYER. *As requested so beautifully by John Donne: "Batter my heart, three-person'd God."*

PARDON my enemies, O Lord; blinded by passion they know not what they do.

—St. Fidelis of Sigmaringen

APR. 24

Compassion for Our Enemies

REFLECTION. We forgive our enemies not because they have asked for forgiveness nor because they deserve it nor because they will stop hurting us. Rather, we recognize that what they have done to us is a symptom of their own brokenness, and the last thing we want to do is make it worse.

We want only to heal them with our love.

PRAYER. *God, please always show a greater love to my enemies than to me, for they need it more.*

HOLY Scripture is so exalted that there is no one in the world wise enough to understand it so fully that his intellect is not overcome by it.

—St. Angela of Foligno

APR. 25

The Mystery of God in Words

REFLECTION. One of the most important tasks of those who study is to know what they do not know. Sacred Scripture, written so long ago in ancient languages, can be very difficult to understand. We have to be careful not to make it say what we want to hear.

We must be like Job who said, "Now I understand that I do not understand, I must trust."

PRAYER. *May I always read and study Sacred Scripture with a profound sense of humility.*

Prayer before reading

Come, Holy Spirit,
fill the hearts of Your faithful.
And kindle in them the fire of Your love.

Prayer after reading

Grant, Lord, that I may be attentive at prayer.
Let my conscience be upright,
my conversation be edifying,
and my whole life be ordered.

Other Titles in this Series

Book No.

141/19 *Praying for Wisdom Every Day*
147/19 *Daily Companion for First Responders*
150/19 *Bible Day by Day*
151/19 *Franciscan Daily Companion*
153/19 *Day by Day with the Mass*
157/19 *Daily Comfort While Grieving*
161/19 *Daily Companion for Caregivers*
162/19 *Day by Day with St. Joseph*
164/19 *Daily Companion for Peace of Heart*
168/19 *Pro-Life Reflections for Every Day*
170/19 *Augustine Day by Day*
175/19 *Minute Meditations from the Popes*
176/19 *Daily Meditations with Saint Augustine*
177/19 *Daily Companion for Men*

YOU don't have to be worthy; you only have to be willing.

—St. Pius of Pietrelcina

APR. 26

We Serve in Our Brokenness

REFLECTION. We often beat ourselves up for not being perfect. We all have our flaws, our shortcomings. Whether these forms of brokenness are because we were born with them or because they are a result of our own sins and mistakes is not important.

God really only expects us to do the best we can with what we are.

PRAYER. *Lord, may I do all I can to serve You.*

IT IS only in adversity that we come to know whether we have made real progress in goodness. —St. Anthony of Padua

APR. 27

The Testing of Our Progress

REFLECTION. We can believe that we are making progress in the spiritual life when everything is going well. We begin to feel good about ourselves. But perhaps only when a difficulty or a crisis occurs can we evaluate the true level of our progress.

The difficulties, far from being a punishment or a curse, can actually be opportunities to purify our motives.

PRAYER. *Lord, purify the motivations of my heart, even if it is through the cross you ask me to carry.*

IT IS wrong for anyone to be anxious to receive more from his neighbor than he himself is willing to give to God.

—St. Francis of Assisi

APR. 28

Putting Things in Perspective

REFLECTION. We normally see things from our own point of view. We want to receive and receive, but we are unwilling to be as generous with others as we would like God to be with us.

The Prayer of St. Francis (probably not written by him, but it evidences his spirit) speaks of not seeking to be consoled, but rather to console.

PRAYER. *Lord, make me an instrument of Your peace.*

PLACE your mind in the softness of life's eternal flow. Place your soul in the brilliance of heaven's endless glow.

—St. Clare of Assisi

APR. 29

Where Our Minds and Our Souls Find Their Home

REFLECTION. We were made for eternity. Thus, we have to be careful not to become so caught up with what is material and passing that we lose track of where our true home lies.

We have to dedicate our minds to what lies beyond—and dedicate our souls to the reality that gives meaning to all that we are.

PRAYER. *May the thoughts of my mind and the depths of my soul find their home in You, O Lord.*

LORD, accept me to the school of Saints to be worthy of You. —Bl. Veronica Antal

APR. 30

Sanctify Me, O Lord

REFLECTION. When we hear the word "Saint," we most often apply it to someone who was incredibly heroic in the Faith. But most Saints are everyday people who continually seek to live the Gospel a little better each day of their lives.

The school of Saints is not just for the elite and super talented; it is for everyone who wants to follow Jesus.

PRAYER. *Lord, may I seek Your holiness. May I strive to be a Saint.*

TO LOVE one's work, in fact, is a divine prerogative: it is likeness to God.

—St. Maximilian Kolbe

MAY 1

Work as a Sharing in the Act of Creation

REFLECTION. The curse that Adam received after the first sin was not to have to work, but that his work would be frustrated.

Work, in itself, is a participation in the act of creation. It is the opportunity to express our own creativity. It also is a way in which we can serve those who depend on the income we receive and those for whom we work.

PRAYER. *May I always see my work as a vocation, a call from You, O Lord.*

A LIGHT does not illumine itself, but instead it diffuses its rays and shines all around upon everything that comes into its view. —St. John of Capistrano

MAY 2

Letting the Light of Christ Shine Through

REFLECTION. If we have received the light of the Wisdom of God, then we have a responsibility to share it with others.

An image used throughout history compares a person to a stained-glass window. We have to let Christ's light shine through us, but we each give that light a tint that is the contribution of our own personality.

PRAYER. *Shine on me, O Lord, with the light of Your Wisdom.*

DO NOT pray for easy lives; pray to be stronger people. —Bl. Solanus Casey

MAY 3

The Lord Is the Source of My Strength

REFLECTION. God wants us to be the most loving people possible. That often means having to face challenges in which we die to ourselves to live for Him and others.

Rather than trying to avoid such challenges, God calls us to embrace them in trust and to ask Him for the grace that we need in order to respond to them with generosity.

PRAYER. *Lord, may You always be my Rock, the source of my fortitude.*

WE ARE mothers of our Lord Jesus Christ when we carry Him in our hearts and in our bodies, lovingly, and with a pure and sincere conscience. —St. Francis of Assisi

MAY 4

Following the Example of Mary

REFLECTION. Mary was the perfect disciple. She saw herself as a humble servant of the Great High King. By saying, "Your will be done," she allowed Jesus to be present in this world.

We do the same thing when we witness to Jesus with our hearts and our bodies. Jesus is once again seen in this world through our witness to His love.

PRAYER. *May I be the humble servant of the Lord.*

SO I am always rejoicing in the Lord. My only complaint is that I do not love him enough. —St. Conrad of Parzham

MAY 5

Inflame My Heart with Love

REFLECTION. We are so often ready to blame others when things do not go the way we would like. That even includes blaming God for our difficulties in the spiritual life.

Maybe we should examine our conscience well and admit that there are things we must change in our lives in order to live more fully in God's love.

PRAYER. *May I love You more today, Lord, and even more tomorrow.*

HUMILITY exists only in those who are poor enough to see that they possess nothing of their own.

—St. Angela of Foligno

MAY 6

Humility and Poverty

REFLECTION. Poverty means that we have nothing of our own. It teaches us that God is the source of all good things and that we have to depend upon His Providence.

This leaves us with a spirit of humility—for this virtue recognizes the fact that without God, we are nothing. We have nothing—except what we receive from Him.

PRAYER. *O Lord, I depend upon You for all I have and am.*

PLACE your labor humbly in the Lord and God will place His grace in thee.

—Bl. Giles of Assisi

MAY 7

Letting God Guide Our Efforts

REFLECTION. If we try to do things by our own efforts, we eventually will either become proud and arrogant when we are successful or frustrated when we fail.

If, on the other hand, we let the Lord guide our efforts and we depend upon His graces, then we will be able to attribute all of our successes to the Lord.

PRAYER. *Not to us, O Lord, but to Your Name belongs the glory.*

MAY 8

ON THIS earth everyone has his cross. But we must act in such a way that we be not the bad, but the good thief.

—St. Pius of Pietrelcina

Making the Choice

REFLECTION. We have a choice when we suffer. We can concentrate on our own sufferings, becoming bitter and resentful as the bad thief did on his cross.

Or we can look around and give comfort to others who are suffering, even those who are suffering because they are sharing our suffering, as the good thief did.

PRAYER. *When I carry my crosses, may I always be like the good thief, O Lord.*

MAY 9

PRAYER is a vessel with which the grace of the Holy Spirit is drawn from that overflowing font of delight, the most blessed Trinity.

—St. Bonaventure

The Outpouring of the Holy Spirit

REFLECTION. In prayer, our voices are lifted up to the Father through the action of the Holy Spirit, but prayer is also the means by which the Holy Spirit showers down graces upon us.

In every dialogue we have with another, we both give and receive, and that also is true of the dialogue of prayer.

PRAYER. *Shower down Your graces upon me, O Spirit of God, so that I might live in Your love.*

EACH of you should love and nourish one another as a mother loves and nourishes her child. —St. Francis of Assisi

MAY 10

Practicing Compassion

REFLECTION. Today we celebrate the commemoration of St. Damien of Molokai who cared for lepers at the cost of his life. Each of us is called to identify the lepers in our lives and to care for them with profound compassion.

This is true for those lepers who suffer from physical illness, but also if they suffer from emotional problems or moral confusion.

PRAYER. *Lord, help me to see who needs my love and care most.*

BE MOVED to pity when you hear or see anyone sin, and praise God because He has delivered you from a like occasion. —Bl. Giles of Assisi

MAY 11

Our Attitude toward Sinners

REFLECTION. It is so easy to see the flaws and sins in others and to condemn them. This is not how Jesus treated sinners in the Gospels. He felt sorry for them—and only wanted to heal them with his love.

It makes little difference whether their brokenness came from life or was self-inflicted. The only thing that matters is that they be healed.

PRAYER. *May I show sinners as much compassion as You have shown me.*

WHEN you encounter difficulties and contradictions, do not try to break them, but bend them with gentleness and time.

—St. Francis de Sales

MAY 12

Little by Little

REFLECTION. We often think that we can change everything with a little bit of effort. The danger is that we can start to do the right thing from wrong motivations and with wrong techniques.

Rather than breaking in the front door, we should go around the house and try to enter through the back door. Gentleness and patience can often do what brute force cannot.

PRAYER. *May my efforts be wise and prudent, O Lord.*

SEEK refuge in Mary because she is the city of refuge. —St. Anthony of Padua

MAY 13

Refuge for Sinners

REFLECTION. In the Gospel of John, Jesus adopts the Beloved Disciple as His brother, giving him the Blessed Virgin as his Mother. The Beloved Disciple is never named in that Gospel, for he is symbolic for each one of us.

We have been made brothers and sisters of Jesus, and the Blessed Virgin Mary is our Mother as well as His.

PRAYER. *O Mary, our Mother, guide and protect the children entrusted to you by your Son.*

HE WHO wishes to have peace and quiet should esteem every person his superior. —Bl. Giles of Assisi

MAY 14

I Am Not Number One

REFLECTION. Who is the most important person in the world? In our lives? Bl. Giles reminds us that we should consider everyone else to be more important than we are.

The question should never be, "How can I make my life more comfortable?" It should be, "What can I do for others to show them how much I respect them?"

PRAYER. *Lord, may I honor and respect all of Your children.*

LET us try to acknowledge, humbly, that many, many mysteries are and will continue to be hidden from us. —St. Maximilian Kolbe

MAY 15

The Limitations of Our Intellect

REFLECTION. It is good to study and reflect upon the mysteries of our Faith, but we have to recognize that they are mysteries—and we will never fully comprehend them.

This does not preclude our accepting these mysteries as an act of faith, for faith is an act of trust. We can trust that what we are hearing is true, even if we cannot understand it.

PRAYER. *Grant me a pliant spirit, O Lord, accepting what I cannot fully understand.*

IN TIMES of desolation, God conceals Himself from us so that we can discover for ourselves what we are without Him.

—St. Margaret of Cortona

MAY 16

The Absence of God

REFLECTION. There are times when we wonder whether God cares and other times when we wonder whether He exists. But when we feel His absence, especially in times of crisis, we realize how desperately we need Him.

It is as if He sometimes steps back so that we can acknowledge that we cannot stand on our own feet. He is our God and our All.

PRAYER. *God, I need You, I love You, I adore You.*

REJOICE and be glad to see yourself enriched by His graces and blessings.

—St. Paschal Baylon

MAY 17

God Is So Good

REFLECTION. There are times when we bemoan the fact that we have not received this or that. We become jealous of those who have the gifts that we would like to have for ourselves.

But rejoicing in how God has blessed us, in great ways and small, is an antidote to this negative attitude. We have to count our blessings and be grateful.

PRAYER. *Thank You, O Lord, for the many, many ways You have blessed me.*

THINK about God Who rejoices the heart and not about vain things which pollute the heart. —St. Felix of Cantalice

MAY 18

Our Thoughts Fixed on Heaven

REFLECTION. When Jesus told the Samaritan woman at the well to call her husband, she responded that she didn't have a husband. She had had five and was living with another man. These represent the gods that the Samaritans had worshiped.

We likewise have a tendency to make gods for ourselves: power, work, prestige, TV, food, drink. God should be the center of our thoughts and our hearts.

PRAYER. *May I reject all the false gods of my life so that You alone, O Lord, might be my God and my All.*

NOTHING is more certain than death, but nothing more uncertain than the hour of our death.

—St. Anthony of Padua

MAY 19

We Know neither the Day nor the Hour

REFLECTION. It seems odd to think about death in May, but we never know how much time any of us will have. It is important to see each moment of our lives as precious, for it is irretrievable.

Now is the time to convert our hearts. Now is the time to make peace where there is conflict.

PRAYER. *Pray for us, Mary, now and at the hour of our death.*

MAY 20

MAY the fiery and honey-sweet power of your love, O Lord, wean me from all things under heaven.

—St. Bernardine of Siena

To Live for Heaven

REFLECTION. God created this world and it is good, but too often it also can distract us from remembering what our true homeland is: heaven.

We have to remind ourselves that what surrounds us is passing, while what calls us is eternity. This puts our desires in perspective, and it helps us to say "No" to what would lead us astray.

PRAYER. *May Your love lead me home, O Lord.*

MAY 21

EVERY creature is a divine word because it proclaims God. —St. Bonaventure

And God Spoke, and It Was Made

REFLECTION. The first account of creation in Genesis tells how God spoke and everything was created. Words were considered to be very powerful in the ancient world. They were not simply symbolic representations of a reality. They made that reality present and alive.

Now, when we look at all of the works of creation, we can hear that powerful word of creation once again.

PRAYER. *Speak Your creative word in my heart, O Lord.*

A SINGLE act of love makes a soul return to life. —St. Maximilian Kolbe

MAY 22

Love Conquers All

REFLECTION. When we choose to sin, we bring a little bit of death into our souls. That death, that evil destroys our spiritual life from the inside.

When we choose to do a good deed, we are choosing love. That love heals the hurt that we have brought upon ourselves by our selfish choices. Love brings our souls back to life.

PRAYER. *Lord, give me the courage to choose love in my life.*

ALL the brothers are to guard against speaking falsely of anyone and are to avoid verbal disputes.

—St. Francis of Assisi

MAY 23

Cautious in Speech

REFLECTION. Speech is so important in building up a community and in tearing it down that St. Francis counseled his followers to be especially careful in what they said about one another.

We often do not know the exact reason why someone is the way that he or she is, and so we should be extremely careful concerning what we say about that person.

PRAYER. *May my words build up the Kingdom. May they be kind and respectful.*

IT IS not enough to love, people have to feel that they are loved. —St. John Bosco

MAY 24

Loving People in Word and Deed

REFLECTION. There are some people who love humanity, but they don't necessarily love individuals. Our love for others has to be real and concrete.

We have to show others respect, especially when they do not respect themselves. We have to spend time and effort on their behalf. We have to treat them how they most need to be treated (whether it be a gentle hug or tough love).

PRAYER. *Give me the wisdom, O Lord, to know how to show my concern and compassion to others.*

ALTHOUGH you feel tepid, approach with confidence, for the greater your infirmity the more you stand in need of a physician. —St. Bonaventure

MAY 25

God the Healer

REFLECTION. There are times when we feel indifferent. We don't have the energy to pray or meditate, or even to care about our spiritual life. It is exactly at these times that we have to strive to overcome our lethargy and reach out.

Our Lord is always there waiting for us, but we have to reach out to Him to let Him heal us.

PRAYER. *Heal me, O Lord, when I am indifferent or depressed or angry, for Your love is truly a balm to my soul.*

GOD does not command us to live in hair shirts and chains, but to love Him above all things and our neighbor as ourselves.

—St. Charles of Sezze

MAY 26

Not Exaggerating Our Spiritual Disciplines

REFLECTION. St. Francis often disciplined his body. He wanted to be totally pure and to drive out every temptation. Later in his life, however, he realized that he had exaggerated his penances, and he apologized to his body for how he had treated it.

We do not need to punish our bodies; we need only to meet well those challenges that come along naturally.

PRAYER. *Purify my heart and my body, O Lord.*

IT IS impossible for virtues to be acquired without solicitude and toil.

—Bl. Giles of Assisi

MAY 27

A Life of Spiritual Discipline

REFLECTION. While virtues are gifts from God, they require an energetic response on our part. We must work at developing and maintaining good habits. This often requires spiritual disciplines—for instance, a good examination of conscience, confession, spiritual direction, or spiritual reading.

Having a healthy spiritual life will help us face our problems.

PRAYER. *Lord, give me the courage and the drive to live a virtuous life.*

A THOUSAND years of enjoying human glory is not worth even an hour spent sweetly communing with Jesus in the Blessed Sacrament. **MAY 28**

—St. Pius of Pietrelcina

Time with Our Best Friend

REFLECTION. Sitting silently before the Blessed Sacrament in a church or chapel seems like private time, possibly even wasted time.

Yet, time spent with our Friend, our Lord, our All, is the most valuable time we can ever spend. It is good for us, for it fosters a deeper relationship with Him.

PRAYER. *Lord Jesus, You are the Bread of Life. You are my God and my All.*

ALTHOUGH we are poor, limited creatures, unable to give Him the glory He deserves, at least let us make an effort to contribute, as far as we can, to give Him the greatest glory possible. —St. Maximilian Kolbe **MAY 29**

Praise the Lord

REFLECTION. God does not need our praise, but it is good for us to dedicate ourselves to that purpose.

Praising another means that we are not seeking our own glory, but rather recognizing the good in the other. Who deserves our praise more than God? God is all good, all knowing, all loving. It is good for us to acknowledge that.

PRAYER. *Praise be to You, O Lord. Let me praise You with all my being.*

MAY 30

A PERSON is really poor in spirit when he hates himself and loves those who strike him in the face.

—St. Francis of Assisi

To Be Poor in Spirit

REFLECTION. This saying of St. Francis almost seems to be masochistic, but it is not. We have to recognize our brokenness and our sinfulness and reject that part of us.

At the same time, we have to recognize that those whom we would normally hate are broken people, and we must want to heal them with our prayer and our love.

PRAYER. *Lord, may I have an honest evaluation of myself and others.*

MAY 31

WE BEG you, Our Lady, exalted above the choirs of Angels that you fill the vessel of our hearts with heavenly grace.

—St. Anthony of Padua

The Visitation

REFLECTION. As the Blessed Virgin Mary brought joy to her cousin Elizabeth, Zechariah, and even to John the Baptist before he was born, so we ask Our Lady to fill our hearts with joy and love.

She intercedes with God that we might receive every grace that will be good for us. She loves us with the same love with which she loved her only Son.

PRAYER. *Blessed are you among women, and blessed is the fruit of your womb, Jesus.*

JUNE 1

WALK the way of the Lord in simplicity. Do not torment your spirit. Say the truth, always the truth.
—St. Pius of Pietrelcina

The Truth, and Nothing but the Truth

REFLECTION. St. Justin the Martyr was a scholar who argued that the Christian Faith was reasonable in the light of the philosophy of the ancient world. He was an apologist, one who defended the truths of the Faith.

In a world in which everything seems to be relative and negotiable, we have to have the courage to defend our Faith when we are called upon to do so.

PRAYER. *Spirit of Truth, guide my thoughts and words and actions.*

JUNE 2

HOW merciful is the Good God in making us dependent upon one another.
—Bl. Solanus Casey

No One Is an Island

REFLECTION. In the First Letter to the Corinthians, St. Paul states that the Holy Spirit has given each of us an outpouring of spiritual gifts (charisms). We are to use these gifts for the good of the community.

No one has received all of the gifts. We therefore must depend on others to supply what is lacking in us.

PRAYER. *Lord, may I never forget how much I need You and others.*

BLESSED be the lovable Lord, Jesus most kind, Who deigns to suffer for us, first in Himself, and then with us and in us....

—St. Bonaventure

JUNE 3

We Never Suffer Alone

REFLECTION. When we are suffering, we feel as if we are on the Cross, looking out, and there is no one there for us. We have to remember Who is on the other side of the Cross.

It is in suffering that we are closest to our Lord. When we suffer with our faith, our passion (suffering) becomes passion (great love).

PRAYER. *Lord, let me die with You so that I might rise with You.*

THERE is no sinner in the world so great whom God cannot in many ways adorn with grace and virtues.

—Bl. Giles of Assisi

JUNE 4

God, Ever Merciful

REFLECTION. When we sin, God does not reject us. We create a rift between us and God, us and each other, and even us and nature.

God is always willing to forgive us, but we have to seek that forgiveness. In other words, God cannot force His love on us; yet, all He wants is that we live in His love.

PRAYER. *Have mercy on me, O Lord, for I am a sinner.*

W HAT you hold, may you always hold. What you do, may you always do and never abandon.

—St. Clare of Assisi

JUNE 5

Persistence in Our Calling

REFLECTION. In our days, it is difficult to make and maintain a permanent commitment. Situations change. People make mistakes. People become bored. There are many reasons why we might want to do something different.

But the Lord calls us to integrity. We have to be consistent, day after day, no matter how the circumstances in which we find ourselves have changed.

PRAYER. *Grant me a joyful persistence in my call, O Lord.*

B LEST is the person who sees the fulfillment of all his good desires.

—St. Anthony of Padua

JUNE 6

The Fulfillment of God's Plan

REFLECTION. If our good desires correspond to God's plans, then we should want to see them fulfilled. The only problem is that we often project upon God what we want to see for our own selfish reasons.

We have to purify our motives to make sure that what we call the Will of God is truly God's Will.

PRAYER. *May I only desire, Lord, that which serves Your Kingdom.*

W**HEN one goes into the missions, one has to be ready for everything.** —Bl. Zbigniew Strzałkowski

JUNE 7

Called to Mission

REFLECTION. Bl. Zbigniew and his confere Bl. Michal were called to the missions in Peru where they were martyred.

Each of us is called to mission, whether at home or on the road. There is no guarantee that things will work out the way we expected, other than if we love, then no matter what happens, the Kingdom will be proclaimed.

PRAYER. *Lord, may I always trust that where You lead me, there I will find You.*

T**HERE is no one whatsoever who can embrace the beloved with so great a love as that wherewith God embraces the soul.** —St. Angela of Foligno

JUNE 8

God's Love for Us

REFLECTION. In our spiritual journey, we often can concentrate too much on what we have to do. It can seem as though we are the only ones in the relationship. It is good to stop and let God love us with His immeasurable compassion.

We would not even know what love was if He had not shown us the true meaning of love on the Cross.

PRAYER. *Let me know, O Lord, how much You truly love me.*

EVERY day He humbles Himself just as He did when He came from His heavenly throne into the Virgin's womb.

—St. Francis of Assisi

JUNE 9

The Eucharist, Sacrament of God's Vulnerability

REFLECTION. In the Sacrament of the Eucharist, Jesus makes Himself available to all who seek Him. The Son of God Who humbled Himself by entering the womb of the Blessed Virgin Mary now enters bread and wine and transforms them to be His own Flesh and Blood.

This is why John's Gospel uses the same word to describe the Incarnation and the Eucharist.

PRAYER. *O Holy Banquet, in which Christ is received, teach me humility.*

THE source of justice is not vengeance but charity. —St. Bridget of Sweden

JUNE 10

Healing the World with Our Love

REFLECTION. St. Thomas Aquinas defined justice as giving each person what that person deserves. The Letter to the Romans extends that definition: it redefines justice as compassion.

The only way to heal the hurt of this world is through love. We destroy the power of evil by choosing to love.

PRAYER. *Lord, may I heal the brokenness of this world with my love.*

THE wearinesses we experience are providential guards against one of the very greatest dangers to holiness—pride.
—Bl. Solanus Casey

JUNE 11

Our Limitations as a Gift

REFLECTION. Our limitations, such as weariness, provide proof that we cannot do certain things by ourselves. We have to reach out to others to help us.

This realization is a bit humbling—which is a good thing. It keeps us from developing a pride-filled tendency to think that we are our own gods.

PRAYER. *Lord, teach me to recognize that I cannot do everything on my own.*

NO ONE can attain to the knowledge of God but by humility. The way to mount high is to descend. —Bl. Giles of Assisi

JUNE 12

The Virtue of Humility

REFLECTION. We all like to be in charge. We all like to think that we are better than others. These are forms of pride. It is God Who has created any good that can be found in us. Others might very well be holier than we are in the eyes of God.

It is when we admit our creatureliness that God can make us like Himself.

PRAYER. *Jesus, root the pride out of my heart; let me be as humble as You are.*

JUNE 13

JESUS Christ feeds us thus every day with Gospel teachings and the Sacraments of the Church. —St. Anthony of Padua

Word and Sacrament

REFLECTION. When we attend Mass, we encounter Jesus in both Word and Sacrament. The readings proclaimed are truly the Word of God. The Eucharist that we receive is truly the Body of Christ.

It is not that one is holier than the other. They both make Christ present to us as they raise us up to the Lord.

PRAYER. *St. Anthony of Padua, pray for us.*

JUNE 14

THERE is never a pilgrim who returns home without one less prejudice and one new idea. —St. Thomas More

On Pilgrimage

REFLECTION. When we travel to lands that have a different culture, we are challenged to see that the way we do things at home is not the only way to do them.

We see how the Holy Spirit blows where It wills, expressing the grace of God in so many varied ways. We are given an opportunity to celebrate the goodness of God's image seen in people who seem very different from us.

PRAYER. *May my every journey fill me with wonder, O Lord.*

EVERY time I hear anyone speak of the Sacred Heart of Jesus or of the Blessed Sacrament I feel an indescribable joy.

—Pope St. John XXIII

JUNE 15

The Body and Heart of Jesus

REFLECTION. The image of the Sacred Heart of Jesus is one of immeasurable love and compassion. He loves us truly to death.

The Holy Eucharist is that love incarnate under the forms of bread and wine. It is a love that becomes one with us when we eat the consecrated host and drink the consecrated wine.

PRAYER. *Lord, may Your love and mine be one.*

I CONSIDER it greater to preserve the good things given by the Lord than to acquire them. **—Bl. Giles of Assisi**

JUNE 16

Exercising Dominion over Creation

REFLECTION. When God gave Adam and Eve dominion over creation, He was not permitting them to exploit what He had created—either for their own selfish purposes or so that they would try to possess those things.

Rather, God wanted them to treat creation with sacred respect, celebrating His goodness as seen through all the things that He had created.

PRAYER. *Teach me true poverty, O Lord, through which I possess nothing but celebrate everything.*

YOU Who surpass man's understanding, make me capable of recognizing Your inestimable burning love by which You emptied Yourself. —St. Angela of Foligno

JUNE 17

Reflecting on the Wonder of God's Love

REFLECTION. St. Paul's Letter to the Philippians speaks of how Jesus emptied Himself of the prerogatives of His Godliness so that He might assume the condition of a slave, even dying on the Cross.

The spiritual life is likewise an emptying of oneself. We are called to remove pride, selfishness, and negative passions from our hearts to fill them with Christ Himself.

PRAYER. *Empty my heart, O Lord, of anything that is not You.*

THE Lord Who made the beginning will take care of the finish.

—St. John of Capistrano

JUNE 18

It Is God Who Guides Us on Our Path

REFLECTION. We have felt the call of God to live in His ways, but the journey seems long and is often difficult. We can become discouraged and wonder what it all means.

We have to trust that God is in charge. Even if things seem to be working out in a strange manner, God can still use what is happening for our good.

PRAYER. *Lead me home, O Lord. Lead me home to You.*

SOMETIMES, by a single hour spent in prayer, more is gained than the whole world....

—St. Bonaventure

JUNE 19

The Power of Prayer

REFLECTION. When God created the world, He did so by words. He said, "Let there be light," and there was light. When we pray, we are using godly words that re-create the world in God's image.

Equally important, our words of prayer re-create our own hearts in God's image. Prayer time is never wasted time. It is one of the most important things we can do in life.

PRAYER. *Lord, teach us how to pray.*

JOY, with peace, is the sister of charity. Serve the Lord with laughter.

—St. Pius of Pietrelcina

JUNE 20

Laughing with the Lord

REFLECTION. At times, when Catholics leave church after Holy Mass, they look as if they had been tortured for the past hour.

We should leave church filled with the love and joy that we have just celebrated by hearing the Word of God and receiving the Eucharist. A smile can be a powerful tool for evangelization.

PRAYER. *Fill my heart with joy, O Lord, so that everyone who sees me will want to find what I have found in You.*

OUR Mother is preparing a very bright way for us; it will also be painful, but victory is always certain.

—St. Maximilian Kolbe

JUNE 21

Mary Calling Us to the Cross

REFLECTION. When Jesus told Mary at the wedding feast at Cana that His hour (the hour of the Cross) had not yet come, she said to the servants to do whatever He told them to do. She was inviting Jesus to carry His Cross.

She likewise invites us to embrace the crosses of our lives, for, as with Jesus, she wants us to be the most loving people possible.

PRAYER. *Mary, please stand by me when I am carrying my cross, as you did for your Son, Jesus.*

YOU wouldn't abandon ship in a storm just because you couldn't control the winds.

—St. Thomas More

JUNE 22

Remaining Faithful to the End

REFLECTION. St. Thomas More was given an impossible choice: to be faithful to the king to whom he had sworn loyalty, or to be faithful to God and His Church. He chose the latter, giving witness to his faith even to the point of death.

We are called to that same fidelity, in small matters as well as in large.

PRAYER. *Lord, keep me always faithful to You and Your Church, no matter what the cost might be.*

DO NOT let the false delights of a deceptive world deceive you. —St. Clare of Assisi

JUNE 23

Renouncing the World

REFLECTION. The world was created to be good, but because of sin, it has become ambiguous. Things that should lead us to God can easily mislead us when we use them guided by our passions.

We have to learn to say "No" to certain things so that we can always say "Yes" to God and His love.

PRAYER. *Only You, O Lord, only You!*

ST. JOHN the Baptist trembled and was afraid even to touch Christ's sacred head. —St. Francis of Assisi

JUNE 24

The Birth of St. John the Baptist

REFLECTION. St. Francis passionately encouraged priests, who daily touch the very Body of Christ, to emulate the humility of St. John the Baptist. He recognized his humble role. He was the precursor and not the Messiah. He was the best man and not the bridegroom.

We, like he, are not to be the center of attention. That role belongs to Christ.

PRAYER. *May I never preach myself, but always point to Jesus, the true Lamb of God.*

BLESSED is that person who does not want to appear in his words and manner save in that way in which Divine Grace has fashioned him. —Bl. Giles of Assisi

JUNE 25

Conforming to Our Divine Call

REFLECTION. God shaped us in His image and likeness. He addressed a call, a vocation, to each of us. He wants us to be the most loving persons possible, to live in His grace.

We find true joy when we conform to what God calls us to be. We find only frustration when we try to impose our own will upon our lives and our future.

PRAYER. *Help me to discern, O Lord, what You want me to do and be.*

DEATH has no terrors for a sincere servant of Christ who is laboring to bring souls to a knowledge of the truth.

—Bl. Raymond Lull

JUNE 26

Willing to Be a Martyr

REFLECTION. There is always a cost to pay when we strive to be Christians. People might misjudge our motives; they might consider us to be foolish; they might accuse us of being frauds.

When we suffer for the sake of the Kingdom, we should rejoice, for it means that God has trusted us enough to invite us into the mystery of the saving Passion of His Son.

PRAYER. *Lord, let me carry the Cross with You.*

I MADE a pact with my tongue not to speak when my heart is disturbed.

—St. Francis de Sales

JUNE 27

Count to Ten

REFLECTION. Some of us have a tendency to say the first thing that comes to mind when we are angry. Others hold in their anger till it explodes, and they end up saying things that cannot be taken back.

We have to find a healthy balance between blurting our hurtful words and repressing them. Virtue is found in the middle.

PRAYER. *Lord, set a guard on what I say to others, especially when I am angry.*

LET your thinking be simple and lowly.

—St. Paschal Baylon

JUNE 28

Being Childlike

REFLECTION. At times, our humanness convinces us that we can know and control everything around us. Yet, when we temper our desire and accept our humanity, we begin to think in a childlike manner—and we learn how to accept whatever comes along.

This doesn't mean that we should not study about our Faith, only that we should do it with humility.

PRAYER. *May I have a childlike faith, O Lord.*

BROTHER Francis and his successors as head of the Order promise obedience and reverence to his holiness Pope Innocent and his successors. —St. Francis of Assisi

JUNE 29

Sts. Peter and Paul

REFLECTION. Franciscans are called to live in obedience. They are to be obedient to God and His calling in their lives. They also are to be obedient to those whom the Lord has chosen to guide His Holy Church.

Obedience is not something that enslaves us, but rather it gives us the opportunity to surrender our will as an act of love.

PRAYER. *Lord, I surrender my will to You and those who exercise Your authority.*

I ALSO fear suffering and especially humiliations, but I brighten up thinking that not even Jesus in the Garden wanted to feel otherwise. —St. Maximilian Kolbe

JUNE 30

The First Martyrs of Rome

REFLECTION. The witness of the martyrdom of the first Christians in Rome had a powerful effect upon the spread of Christianity. As Tertullian said, "The blood of the Martyrs is the seed of the Church."

We, too, are called to give witness, for the world desperately needs to see a living proclamation of the Faith.

PRAYER. *Give me courage, O Lord, when I am called to give witness in small ways and great.*

IF THE Lord grants me eternal happiness, I shall pray for all and for the conversion of so many whom I leave unconverted.

—St. Junípero Serra

JULY 1

The Intercession of the Saints

REFLECTION. In a flight of fancy, we might picture heaven as being an eternal vacation destination where all our needs and wants are met without any effort on our part.

But Saints work, interceding for those who need it, just as the Blessed Virgin Mary intercedes for us, and as do all the Saints to whom we reach out with our prayers.

PRAYER. *St. Junípero Serra, pray for us.*

YOU are holy, Lord, the only God, and Your deeds are wonderful. —St. Francis of Assisi

JULY 2

Holy, Holy, Holy

REFLECTION. In the Bible, holy means totally other. God is holy, for He is so far beyond our understanding. God is so great, so wonderful, so magnificent that we cannot even begin to comprehend the extent of His qualities.

We stand before the Holy One with a sense of childlike awe, filled with a sense of wonder.

PRAYER. *I praise You, O Lord, with all my being.*

REGRET not that which is past; and trust not to thine own righteousness.

—St. Anthony of Padua

JULY 3

The Feast of St. Thomas

REFLECTION. St. Thomas has been remembered throughout history as being doubtful. Yet, he used his doubts to come to a deeper, more profound faith that led him to proclaim, "My Lord and my God!" This is one of the most powerful professions of faith found in the Gospels.

Like St. Thomas, we have to get past our mistakes, trusting in God's mercy alone.

PRAYER. *My Lord and my God; my God and my All.*

TASTE the hidden sweetness that lies within your heart which God has kept for those whose lives are tender within.

—St. Clare of Assisi

JULY 4

How God Loves Us

REFLECTION. At times, it is good to take stock of our interior life. If we have worked at our conversion and prayed, done penitential practices and charity, and lived virtuously, then we will have done all that we should have done.

But there is another part of the spiritual life in which it is not we who act, but God, Who fills our hearts with His consolation.

PRAYER. *Let me meet You in my heart, O Lord.*

MAKE the good of others thine own, if it pleases you; and make the evil of others your concern, if it displeases you. —Bl. Giles of Assisi

JULY 5

Responding to Good and Bad

REFLECTION. If others are doing things that are good, then we should celebrate the good things they are doing. We should not be jealous of them or minimize what they have done.

If they are doing bad things, we should be concerned for them because their actions indicate their hurt. We should pray for their healing.

PRAYER. *Lord, may the way I respond to others show that I only want the Kingdom of God to grow.*

LORD, help me, because I perish. Kept in your heart, I am in a safe place.
—Bl. Veronica Antal

JULY 6

Safe in the Lord

REFLECTION. In the Book of Revelation, we read the symbolic message that the enemy might kill us but will never harm us. God does not always intervene to rescue us from our difficulties, or even from our disasters—but He never abandons us.

We will never suffer alone. Jesus will always unite our cross with His.

PRAYER. *Lord, I place my trust in You, for You are my Rock and my Fortress.*

FRANCIS saw Christ's image in every poor person he met and he was prepared to give them everything he had. —St. Bonaventure

JULY 7

Serving the Poor

REFLECTION. We have been blessed by the Lord so that we might share our abundance with those who most need it. Tertullian said that what was in excess was robbed from the poor.

In reality, we should not expect the poor to be grateful to us for what we have done. We should be grateful to them for having given us the opportunity to share our love with them.

PRAYER. *My Lord Jesus, may I always see Your face in the poor.*

GOD is the one who leads me and elevates me to that state.

—St. Angela of Foligno

JULY 8

God Is in Charge

REFLECTION. We should be cautious about taking credit for our growth in the spiritual life. Doing so could lead us to think that we are in charge. It is God Who calls, Who gives us the desire to respond to the call, and Who gives us the strength to surrender to that same call.

God is the One Who began the process, and He will bring it to completion.

PRAYER. *God, You are the potter; I am the clay.*

THE best gift anyone can give a friend is to pray for him. —Bl. Solanus Casey

JULY 9

The Power of Prayer

REFLECTION. At times, we might feel as if we would like to do something for another, but the only thing that we can do is pray for that person. We should not denigrate the power of our prayer.

When we pray, our love is joined to God's love and that love embraces the person for whom we are praying—and love always changes reality.

PRAYER. *Loving God, I pray for* N. *who is need. May my love and Yours truly embrace him/her.*

A MORSEL of pure suffering gives such strength that you could almost do crazy things. —St. Veronica Giuliani

JULY 10

Holy Foolishness

REFLECTION. Those who are in love often do things that seem foolish. We could see suffering not as a curse, but rather as a blessing—a sharing in the Passion of Christ. We could see suffering not as something that isolates us, but as something that connects us to the Person for Whom we offer it.

While these ideas don't seem logical, they make absolute sense in the mystical world.

PRAYER. *I thank You, Lord, for the crosses of my life.*

HATRED is not a creative force. Love alone creates. —St. Maximilian Kolbe

JULY 11

Choosing Love Instead of Hate

REFLECTION. When St. Maximilian Kolbe was imprisoned in Auschwitz, a fellow prisoner asked him if they should not hate the Nazis for what they were doing to them. He responded that they should not hate, for hate is a destructive force. Only love is creative.

Love destroys the power of evil that, by definition, is the absence of love and goodness.

PRAYER. *Lord, let me always choose to love, even when surrounded by hate.*

YOU, O Lord, are courage, You are our haven and our hope. —St. Francis of Assisi

JULY 12

The Lord Is a Safe Refuge in Time of Need

REFLECTION. We can find ourselves in confusing situations in which we are not really sure how to proceed. The easiest discernments are between good and evil. The more difficult ones are between good and better and bad and worse.

God is the One Who will guide us. He will help us make the right choice and give us the courage to move forward.

PRAYER. *Guide me, O Lord, for in You I take refuge.*

LET us couple patience and long-suffering in the spirit of meekness and faith.

—St. Anthony of Padua

JULY 13

Waiting for the Lord

REFLECTION. We live in a society of instant gratification. If the computer takes ten seconds to reboot, we become impatient and agitated. Yet, waiting and patience are necessary in the spiritual life.

They remind us that we are not in control. They give us time to reflect and purify our motives. They teach us to surrender to God's Will and God's time.

PRAYER. *Lord, teach me to wait with supreme patience.*

TO CULTIVATE piety and kindness is a work fruitful above every other work.

—Bl. Giles of Assisi

JULY 14

To God and to Neighbor

REFLECTION. Piety means to give to God what is His due. It is a sense of reverence and submission to His Will. Kindness is what we give to our neighbor. It is treating that person with exaggerated respect.

Our faith must have both the vertical dimension addressed to God and the horizontal dimension addressed to our neighbor.

PRAYER. *Lord, may I be both pious and kind.*

HUMAN desire does not tend to anything that is not either the Supreme Good, or a means to it, or a reflection of it.

—St. Bonaventure

JULY 15

The Supreme Good, Which is God

REFLECTION. We often experience strong desires that are actually passions. True desire is what seeks the only thing that will satisfy our deepest, most profound need.

God placed that need, that hunger in our hearts so that we might reach out to Him with all that we are—with as much zeal as He reaches out to us.

PRAYER. *Teach me, O Lord, to seek You with all that I am.*

THE more a soul becomes like Immaculata, the more it becomes mother of Jesus in its heart, in a supernatural fashion. —St. Maximilian Kolbe

JULY 16

Mary, Model of Holiness

REFLECTION. The Blessed Virgin Mary is the model of what we should become in our spiritual life. Like her, we have to be open to the invitation of God to make the presence of Jesus real in the world.

While we do not have the special graces that she did, we can do the best we can with those graces that each of us has received.

PRAYER. *Our Lady of Mount Carmel, pray for us.*

DO NOT lose your inner peace for anything whatsoever, even if your whole world seems upset. —St. Francis de Sales

JULY 17

Peace in the Midst of Chaos

REFLECTION. It is not easy to remain calm when things seem to be falling apart around us. Yet, when we remember that God is in charge, it helps.

We also have to remember that God can make good come out of even terrible situations (such as the Cross). This helps us realize that no matter how bad something seems, God can change it for the good.

PRAYER. *Calm my spirit, O Lord, and help me to maintain my peace.*

IF YOU do not strive, you cannot overcome sin. —Bl. Veronica Antal

JULY 18

Committing Oneself to Conversion

REFLECTION. It is not always easy to say "No" to those parts of our lives that fall short of what they should be. This is true especially if we have formed bad habits that have become second nature to us.

Yet, if we truly love the Lord, then we will invest our efforts in the task of purifying our hearts so that God might reside in them fully.

PRAYER. *Lord, I will do everything I can—everything I must—to open my heart to You.*

W HEREVER we go, won't we have Our Lord in the Blessed Sacrament with us? Isn't that enough to make us happy?

—Bl. Solanus Casey

JULY 19

Our Lord Is Always There

REFLECTION. Change can often cause anxiety because we do not know what awaits us. This is true especially when we have to move from where we call home.

Bl. Solanus reminds us that our true home is Christ, and every time we receive the Eucharist, we are at home with our Lord—wherever we happen to find ourselves.

PRAYER. *You are my home, O Lord, and wherever I might be, there I am at home in You.*

W HAT a man is before God, that he is and no more.

—St. Francis of Assisi

JULY 20

Our Value before the Lord

REFLECTION. When each of us tries to determine our value as a person, we can exaggerate: either by being unrealistically positive, seeing ourselves as all but perfect, or by being unrealistically negative, seeing ourselves as total failures.

We have to look at ourselves through the eyes of God. We are broken, we are sinners, but we also are loved beyond limit.

PRAYER. *Let me see myself always, O Lord, as You see me.*

THE Word of God is a light to the mind and fire to the will. It enables man to know God and to love Him.

—St. Lawrence of Brindisi

JULY 21

Light and Fire

REFLECTION. One of the attributes of Franciscan Spirituality is the belief that the Word of God speaks directly to each of us. In fact, St. Francis opened the Gospels three times to discern how he and his followers were to live their lives.

We all need to read and meditate upon the Word of God if we, too, wish to know what He wants of us.

PRAYER. *Lord, may Your Word speak directly to my mind and heart.*

BECAUSE of love, and in it, the soul first grows tender; then it pines and grows weak, and afterward finds strength.

—St. Angela of Foligno

JULY 22

The Stages of the Spiritual Life

REFLECTION. We should not expect our relationship with God to be static. Every relationship changes with time. There are periods when we will feel more consolation, and there are periods when that consolation will be withdrawn.

At times, we will be drawn to this relationship with all we have and are; other times we will experience a dryness. The important thing is never to give up.

PRAYER. *Send Your Holy Spirit of love into my heart, O Lord, so that I might live and die in You.*

JULY 23

THERE is no sinner in the world, however much at enmity with God, who cannot recover God's grace by recourse to Mary. —St. Bridget of Sweden

Advocate of Sinners

REFLECTION. The Blessed Virgin Mary has always invited people to follow her Son. She directs this invitation especially toward those who are estranged through their sinfulness.

Mary considers herself to be their Mother as well, and she cannot stand to see their suffering (even if they have brought that suffering upon themselves through their sins).

PRAYER. *Mary, please pray for those who do not have recourse to you.*

JULY 24

DO YOU wish to grow in holiness? Do not toil concerning yourself nor the world and in this way you will be poor. —St. Anthony of Padua

Setting Priorities

REFLECTION. If we live for our own benefit, we will get lost in our own desires. If we live for things of this world, we will use all our energy to amass more and more and never be satisfied.

If we toil for the Kingdom of God, then we might not have many possessions, but we actually will have everything we need in the Lord.

PRAYER. *Everything for the Kingdom, Lord; nothing for myself.*

LIFE begins to make sense when we recognize and acknowledge God's infinite goodness and our absolute dependence on Him. —St. Maximilian Kolbe

JULY 25

The True Meaning of Life

REFLECTION. Why am I here? How can I live the best life possible? These questions cannot be answered without reference to God's plan for each one of us to live in His love.

Yet, we also have to recognize that we cannot possibly follow that plan on our own, for we are too broken to truly respond to His love without His help.

PRAYER. *Lord, may I live as You would have me live.*

GREAT occasions for serving God come seldom, but little ones surround us daily. —St. Francis de Sales

JULY 26

Sts. Joachim and Anne, Grandparents of Jesus

REFLECTION. On this commemoration of the grandparents of Jesus, we are reminded that the role of grandparents is usually not to do spectacular things. Rather, they often do simple things that make all the difference in the world to their grandchildren.

We have to seize the opportunities that life inherently presents to us to consecrate our everyday actions.

PRAYER. *May all I say, all I do, be consecrated in Your love.*

STRIVE to acquire purity of conscience so you may feel what is opposed to your soul.

—Bl. Giles of Assisi

JULY 27

Purifying Our Conscience

REFLECTION. We purify our conscience by slowly stripping away any trace of selfishness and sinfulness. This is a process that requires examination, prayer, and study. The Holy Spirit helps us to slowly identify and eliminate any problematic areas.

When our conscience is pure, we will be able to make clear and profound choices on how to follow God's Will.

PRAYER. *Holy Spirit, help me to delve into the depths of my conscience to purify it in the light of Your love.*

NOTHING should be repulsive to the servant of God but sin.

—St. Francis of Assisi

JULY 28

Humble Service

REFLECTION. There are tasks that we might consider beneath our dignity, possibly because they are dirty or difficult or messy. If we are doing them out of our love for the Lord, then even the most humble work could be seen as having great dignity.

Only selfishness and sin should disgust us, for these things are truly ugly, truly repulsive.

PRAYER. *May all I do be done in Your Name and Your Love.*

W E BECOME what we love and who we love shapes what we become. —St. Clare of Assisi

JULY 29

The Lover and the Beloved

REFLECTION. Both St. Francis and St. Clare spoke of their relationship with Christ as a spousal relationship. Love impelled them to leave all to follow Christ.

Love so transformed them that St. Francis came to look like the beloved when he received the Stigmata, and St. Clare saw Christ and herself in the image she saw in the mirror of the Cross.

PRAYER. *Lord, hide my heart in Your love.*

F RANCIS' whole soul went out to the sick and the poor, and where he could not offer material assistance he lavished his affection. —St. Bonaventure

JULY 30

Those Who Need Our Help and Compassion

REFLECTION. St. Francis always had compassion for those who needed his help. He treated them with a sacred dignity, not only giving them the material things they sought, but also building up their self-esteem by treating them with respect.

We are surrounded by people who need our help, even if it is simply spending time listening to their problems.

PRAYER. *Lord, open my eyes to recognize those who need my help.*

WOE to me if I should prove myself but a halfhearted soldier in the service of my thorn-crowned Captain. —St. Fidelis of Sigmaringen

JULY 31

A Soldier for Christ

REFLECTION. St. Ignatius of Loyola began his adult life as a soldier, but after a severe injury he heard the call of Jesus and formed the Jesuits, becoming a soldier for Christ.

God often places desires and talents in our hearts, which we carefully must discern and purify so that we use them as God intended.

PRAYER. *May I do all for the greater honor and glory of God.*

HOLINESS consists of things that are within the reach of everyone. Nobody is told scourge yourselves, fast, go into ecstasy.

—Bl. Andrea Giacinto Longhin

AUG. 1

The Simplicity of Holiness

REFLECTION. At times, we believe that to be holy means to live an extraordinary life filled with supernatural phenomena. Rarely is this true.

Most truly holy people live ordinary, everyday existences filled with extraordinary love. They might not be famous or even known outside of their immediate circle of friends, but their commitment to do what is right and good makes them truly holy.

PRAYER. *Lord, teach me to be holy as You are holy.*

IF ANYONE does not wish to have Mary Immaculate for his Mother, he will not have Christ for his Brother. —St. Maximilian Kolbe

AUG. 2

The Feast of the Portiuncula

REFLECTION. The Church and the title of Our Lady of the Angels were especially dear to St. Francis. He considered the Church to be the home of his followers. He considered Our Lady to be their Mother and model and guide.

This is why Franciscans have always considered Mary to be the Queen of the Franciscan Order.

PRAYER. *Mary, Queen of the Franciscan Order and Our Lady of the Angels, pray for us.*

THE more the soul receives consolations and feels God, the more its love grows, but the more it pines in the absence of the Beloved.

—St. Angela of Foligno

AUG. 3

Holy Desire

REFLECTION. The Lord plants His love in our hearts, and that love binds us to Him. When we don't feel His consolation, we experience a holy longing to be one with Him again.

This separation can be caused by our own negligence, or it can be a gift from the Lord so that our relationship is not based solely on the consolation we receive from Him.

PRAYER. *I long to be one with You, O Lord.*

FIX your eyes on Heaven; it is there that your hearts will find that which will satisfy them completely. —St. John Vianney

AUG. 4

The Focus of Our Lives

REFLECTION. The love of Christ is the only love that will truly satisfy the deepest hunger of our hearts. Every other love will fall short—as people make mistakes or go away.

Only the love of Christ is eternal. Only His love will heal us. Therefore, we must live with our bodies here on earth, but with our hearts in heaven.

PRAYER. *Lord, may I always remember where my true home is.*

BLEST is the womb of the glorious Virgin because for nine months, it bore the All Good, the Highest Good, the Delight of angels, the Reconciliation of sinners.

—St. Anthony of Padua

AUG. 5

Mary, the Perfect Disciple

REFLECTION. When a woman in the crowd shouted out a blessing upon the womb that bore Jesus and the breasts that fed Him, He responded that more blessed is that person who hears the Word of God and keeps it.

Mary is truly blessed for she cared for Jesus. Her spiritual Motherhood made her a disciple of her own Son.

PRAYER. *Mary, Mother of Jesus, pray for us.*

O HIGHEST Love, Immense Love, Eternal Love, Infinite Love.

—St. Francis Anthony Fasani

AUG. 6

The Transfiguration

REFLECTION. During the Transfiguration, God rolled back the mystery of the identity of Christ for just a moment so that the disciples might understand His true Self. This prepared them for the Passion.

We experience that same revelation in our own lives when we allow ourselves to reflect upon and enter into His love.

PRAYER. *May we, like You, Jesus, be the Father's beloved.*

O BLESSED poverty, how beloved by God, how safe in the world, do you make those who love you.

—St. Bonaventure

AUG. 7

Poverty as Our Refuge

REFLECTION. St. Bonaventure recognized that there are many temptations in the world that can lead us away from total surrender to the Will of God.

Poverty, therefore, serves as a safeguard against this danger—for as we abandon things and attitudes, we find ourselves freer to be able to abandon ourselves to the Lord.

PRAYER. *Lord, make me poor so that I might be rich in You.*

PRAYER is the beginning and the end of all good. —Bl. Giles of Assisi

AUG. 8

Prayer, the Source and the Goal

REFLECTION. Prayer awakens our desire to serve God and to serve our neighbor. It gives us the strength to do this well. It keeps us constant to the commitment that we have made in regard to service.

It consecrates our work, making it holy in the love of the Lord. It brings us to thanksgiving for having had the opportunity to give of ourselves.

PRAYER. *May prayer always lead me out and bring me home again.*

HAIL, Queen Wisdom! The Lord save you, with your sister, pure, holy Simplicity. —St. Francis of Assisi

AUG. 9

St. Teresa Benedicta of the Cross

REFLECTION. St. Teresa Benedicta, Edith Stein, sought the Wisdom of God in great philosophical studies and in the simplicity of contemplation in a Carmelite monastery.

Wisdom and learning do not have to make us complicated and arrogant. In fact, they should do the exact opposite, making us so simple that we become childlike in our embrace of the mystery of God's love.

PRAYER. *May the use of my talents never lead me to arrogance, but rather to true simplicity.*

I HAVE nothing to hide; if they come, we are going to give witness to the truth.

—Bl. Zbigniew Strzałkowski

AUG. 10

St. Lawrence, the Martyr

REFLECTION. When St. Lawrence was called before a Roman official and ordered to deny his faith, he refused. He had to be a faithful witness to who he was and what he believed—no matter what it cost him.

We, each day, are asked to give witness to who we are and what we believe. We have to be willing to pay the price.

PRAYER. *Give me the courage, O Lord, to give faithful witness to You.*

GAZE upon the Lord; Gaze upon His face; Gaze upon the One Who holds you in His embrace. Gaze upon His life. Gaze upon His love.

—St. Clare of Assisi

AUG. 11

Keeping Christ before Our Eyes

REFLECTION. St. Clare recognized that the eyes are the doors to our souls. If we gaze upon the one whom we love, our love for that person will grow.

One need only think of two young lovers on a park bench, unable to take their eyes off of each other. Would that this would be true of us and Christ!

PRAYER. *Lord, may I see Your face today, and every day of my life.*

SON [of God], Wisdom of the Father, grant me light and make me wise.

—St. Paschal Baylon

AUG. 12

Jesus, Wisdom Incarnate

REFLECTION. In the early days of the Church, Christians tried to figure out how Jesus could have existed before He was born in Bethlehem. One of their best solutions to this question was to say that He was God's Wisdom incarnate.

Whenever one spoke of the figure of Wisdom in the Old Testament, the writer was really speaking about Jesus without even knowing it.

PRAYER. *Jesus, source and goal of Wisdom, have mercy on us.*

IF A tiny spark of God's love already burns within you, do not expose it to the wind for it may get blown out...stay quiet with God.

—St. Charles Borromeo

AUG. 13

Protecting Our Spiritual Life

REFLECTION. We have to be careful to shield the spark of God's Wisdom and life within our hearts. It is so easy to become distracted by the things of the world. We could easily let that spark be blown out by the winds of temptation.

We have to be prudent in what we watch, what we read, what we discuss—all we do—to protect our spiritual life.

PRAYER. *May my spiritual life teach me to rest in You, O Lord.*

JESUS loves greatly those who imitate Him in love toward His most pure Mother. —St. Maximilian Kolbe

AUG. 14

Devotion to the Immaculate

REFLECTION. St. Maximilian Kolbe taught all throughout his life that it was essential to pass through Mary to come to Jesus. She, being the most loving of God's creatures, is our most powerful intercessor—but also the one who reveals to us what it truly means to be a disciple of Christ.

The Blessed Mother, through her surrender to God's call, made Christ present in this world.

PRAYER. *Hail Mary, full of grace, the Lord is with thee.*

HAIL, His Palace. Hail, His Tabernacle. Hail, His Robe. Hail, His Handmaid. Hail, His Mother. —St. Francis of Assisi

AUG. 15

The Assumption

REFLECTION. The Blessed Virgin Mary must have been heartbroken when her Son died on the Cross. She must have been overjoyed when He rose. Then He ascended into heaven.

Although she would have met Him in Word and Sacrament, one can picture her longing so much to hold Him again that one day God released her from the bonds of this world.

PRAYER. *Mary, assumed into Heaven, pray for us.*

I DO not expect a high place in heaven. I will be very grateful to have a little corner where I can love God for all eternity.

—St. Marianne Cope

AUG. 16

Humbly in Heaven

REFLECTION. Heaven should not be viewed as a place where our every desire will be fulfilled. Rather, it will be a continuation and a purification of what we already are doing on earth.

The Blessed Virgin Mary—whose Assumption into heaven we celebrated yesterday—continues to intercede for her children there. Like her, we will continue to do good in heaven.

PRAYER. *May I view my service of others here on earth as a foreshadowing of heaven.*

THE most beautiful act of faith is the one made in darkness, in sacrificing, and with extreme effort.

—St. Pius of Pietrelcina

AUG. 17

Trusting beyond Trust

REFLECTION. There are times when we are called to do the right thing, but we do not feel the consolation of the Lord or even His presence when we are doing it.

This was true of St. Teresa of Calcutta, who for many, many years of her life served the poorest of the poor—while she herself was suffering from an incredible spiritual darkness.

PRAYER. *Give me strength, O Lord, even if I don't know where I will find the strength to do the right thing.*

ATTRIBUTE to God every good you have received. Otherwise, you will be guilty of theft. —St. Anthony of Padua

AUG. 18

God Is the Source and Goal of All Good Things

REFLECTION. It is futile to claim credit for anything that we have or have done. What we have is a gift from God, and what we have done could not have been done without His grace.

This is why St. Paul writes in First Corinthians that if we are to boast, we should boast in the Lord. Without Him, we would be nothing and could no nothing.

PRAYER. *Thank You, Lord, for what I am and for what You have given me.*

PURITY of heart seeks God, devotion espouses Him. —Bl. Giles of Assisi

AUG. 19

Stages in the Spiritual Life

REFLECTION. There are different stages in the spiritual life. We first must seek God. The only way we can do this is by emptying our hearts of every other desire—and especially of distractions.

This eventually leads us to practices of devotion by which our love for God grows and leads to union of His Heart with ours.

PRAYER. *May my love for You grow, O Lord, until we are one.*

ST. FRANCIS had an extraordinary meekness, not only toward other people, but also toward animals. —St. Bonaventure

AUG. 20

The Meek Shall Inherit the Earth

REFLECTION. To be meek is to seek to treat everyone and everything with profound respect. It means that one does not seek to be superior to the other, to have power over it. It means seeing and judging everything as God does—and seeking to honor and celebrate it.

The meek, because they do not seek to possess the earth, are capable of inheriting it.

PRAYER. *Heal me of my arrogance, O Lord. Make me meek toward all.*

HOLY Communion is the shortest and safest way to heaven. —Pope St. Pius X

AUG. 21

Heaven Begun and Heaven Promised for the Future

REFLECTION. The Holy Eucharist is the presence of the Body and Blood of Jesus. When we partake of Holy Communion, the Flesh of Jesus and our flesh become one.

We are living in His love here on earth. But the Eucharist is also a promise that we will be one with Him in the future—in heaven.

PRAYER. *Body of Christ, save me. Blood of Christ, inebriate me.*

HAIL, holy Lady, most holy Queen, Mother of God, Mary who art every Virgin. —St. Francis of Assisi

AUG. 22

Mary, Queen of Heaven and Earth

REFLECTION. At the Wedding Feast of Cana, Mary informed Jesus about the lack of wine. In a sense, she was preparing the wedding feast.

In the Old Testament, that was the role of the Queen Mother. The queen was not the wife of the king (for he had many), but rather his mother. Mary is being presented as the Queen Mother, the Queen of heaven and earth.

PRAYER. *Hail, Holy Queen, Mother of Mercy.*

BY VIRTUE of love is the lover transformed in the beloved and the beloved transformed in the lover. —St. Angela of Foligno

AUG. 23

The Two Shall Become One

REFLECTION. All throughout the Gospel of John there is a constant invitation to fall in love with God. Our relationship should not be one of an acquaintance (a distant rapport), or even one of a friendship (a more intimate relationship, but yet in some ways limited).

We are called to be in love with God, for God is already in love with us.

PRAYER. *Lord, may I love You without limit, and may I open my heart fully to receive Your love.*

WALK with your feet on earth, but in your heart be in heaven.

—St. John Bosco

AUG. 24

Practical and Yet Spiritual

REFLECTION. In our Christian life, we must be practical in the way we try to live our lives. This requires a certain prudence and forethought.

Yet, we cannot allow the concerns of this world to make us lose track of our ultimate goal. We have to evaluate our everyday activities in light of their higher, spiritual values.

PRAYER. *Lord, may I live in today—with my eyes set on tomorrow.*

BE KINDLY disposed toward the poor, the wretched and afflicted; help them as much as you can and console them.

—St. Louis IX, King

AUG. 25

Those Who Have Been Put in Charge

REFLECTION. We all exercise some form of authority: possibly at work, in our family, among our friends.

This authority has been given to us so that we might use it in the service of those who most need our help. The advice that St. Louis gave to his son and successor is still valid for each of us today.

PRAYER. *Lord, may I use every gift, every ability You have given me in the service of others.*

HOW happy is he who lives in You, Lord. O, sweet bond that unites me to Jesus.

—Bl. Veronica Antal

AUG. 26

May I Be One with You

REFLECTION. Bl. Veronica, whose feast we celebrate today, was not an extraordinary person. She was faithful, helpful, sincere. But when faced with a crisis that threatened her life, she remained faithful to her deeply held values.

We are called to give witness to our faith and values on an everyday basis as well as in times of crisis—when we are asked to give our all.

PRAYER. *Lord, may I hold firm to the values that give witness to Your love.*

CHRIST acts like a loving mother. To induce us to follow Him, He gives us Himself as an example and promises us a reward in His Kingdom.

—St. Anthony of Padua

AUG. 27

Loved with a Mother's Love

REFLECTION. St. Monica, the mother of St. Augustine, gives us a prime example of a mother's love for her child. She never gave up on him when he was still a pagan.

She continually prayed for him, giving him an example of a good Christian life, speaking of the rewards God holds for the faithful. In all of this, she reflects how Jesus treats every one of us.

PRAYER. *I know that You never give up on me, Lord. Please make sure I do not give up on myself.*

NEVER confuse your mistakes with your value as a human being.

—St. Francis de Sales

AUG. 28

We All Make Mistakes

REFLECTION. None of us is perfect. We all make mistakes. Think of St. Augustine whose feast we celebrate today. He searched for God in so many places before he finally realized that God was already in his heart.

He said, "Late have I loved Thee." Yet, what is important is not how long it took him to turn to the Lord—but that he did.

PRAYER. *May I always remember the words of St. Augustine, "There is no Saint without a past, no sinner without a future."*

[JESUS,] whose fragrance will revive the dead, whose glorious vision will be the happiness of all the citizens of the heavenly Jerusalem. —St. Clare of Assisi

AUG. 29

Heading to Heaven

REFLECTION. Notice that St. Clare does not speak of heaven as being a place or an activity. Heaven is seen as a relationship with Our Lord Jesus Christ.

This relationship is so profound and life giving that even the dead would rise from the grave. It would create a community, a heavenly Jerusalem, in which every division and hurt created by sin would be wiped away.

PRAYER. *Lead me home to You, O Lord. Come, Lord Jesus.*

ST. FRANCIS was a mirror and a shining example of Christian perfection, but in his own eyes he was only a sinner.

—St. Bonaventure

AUG. 30

Our Own Estimation

REFLECTION. St. Francis often spoke of how he was the greatest of sinners. Given his holiness, that might seem to be a gross exaggeration.

Yet, given the graces that he had received from the Lord, maybe it was useful for his spiritual life for him to see how he had fallen short of what he could have been.

PRAYER. *May I not lose track of my sinfulness and brokenness.*

LET your words be few and useful and thoughtful.

—Bl. Giles of Assisi

AUG. 31

Well-Chosen Words

REFLECTION. While the Franciscans have never vowed total silence, they have recognized the danger of speaking to excess, especially by using thoughtless and hurtful words against each other. We should speak little, listen always, and seek to understand.

Words are powerful. We should use them to build up the Kingdom of God, and not simply to entertain ourselves.

PRAYER. *May every word I speak be well chosen and constructive.*

PURE and holy Simplicity puts all the learning of this world, all natural wisdom, to shame. —St. Francis of Assisi

SEPT. 1

Simple vs. Complicated

REFLECTION. Studying our Faith, developing programs, and making great plans are not in themselves wrong. The difficulty arises when we allow these activities to take control of our lives—especially our spiritual lives.

We are called to childlike simplicity, even in the midst of these efforts. Simplicity refuses to complicate the mysteries of our Faith; it simply celebrates them.

PRAYER. *Grant me the true Wisdom of Your Heart, Lord Jesus.*

THIS whole world is full of God! —St. Angela of Foligno

SEPT. 2

Where Are You, O Lord?

REFLECTION. We sometimes ask where God is. The answer is that He is everywhere! It is not a matter of God somehow hiding from us.

Rather, we are not looking around with the eyes of faith. When we do this, we see that He is present in Sacrament and Word, in the Church, in our families, in nature—indeed in all places and in all things.

PRAYER. *Lord, open the eyes of my faith so that I might see Your presence everywhere.*

SEPT. 3

ALTHOUGH not everyone loves the truth, yet only truth can be the basis for lasting happiness.

—St. Maximilian Kolbe

The Truth Will Set Us Free

REFLECTION. Some will argue that the truth is relative, that it depends upon one's gender or ethnic background or religion or social circumstances. But the truth is one, and it is eternal.

We might find different ways of expressing the truth in our own times and circumstances, but that does not change the fact that the truth, itself, does not change.

PRAYER. *Lord Jesus, You are the way, and the truth, and the life.*

SEPT. 4

APART from the Cross, there is no other ladder by which we may get to heaven.

—St. Rose of Viterbo

Embracing the Cross

REFLECTION. In her short life, St. Rose of Viterbo embraced a life of penitential practices.

Carrying our crosses—whether caused by events out of our control or due to penitential practices that we adopt (e.g., fasting, periods of solitude and prayer, controlling our speech)—is the only way to die to ourselves so that we might live in Christ.

PRAYER. *Lord, may I die to myself often so that I might live in and for You.*

LET me make best use of the fleeting moments. They will not return.

—St. Marianne Cope

SEPT. 5

Time Is Precious

REFLECTION. We have no idea when the end of the world will happen. We do not know when our own personal end will occur. We have to embrace each moment as precious.

It is sad when people miss a precious moment of grace, or when they wait too long to say or do what should have been said or done long ago. Today—now—is the time to act.

PRAYER. *May I use each moment of my life both as a precious gift to myself and a precious offering to You.*

WE DO not go to Holy Communion because we are good; we go to become good. **—St. John Bosco**

SEPT. 6

The Eucharist Leads Us to Holiness

REFLECTION. Before we receive the Eucharist, we say that we are not worthy for the Lord to enter under our roof, and this is true.

But the love that we receive when we partake of the Eucharist helps heal our unworthiness. It gives us the courage and fortitude to live up to what we say we are. It calls us to true holiness.

PRAYER. *O Lord, I am not worthy.*

HIDE nothing from your confessor...a sick man can be cured only by revealing his wounds.

—St. Margaret of Cortona

SEPT. 7

Total Transparency

REFLECTION. We might be a bit embarrassed to confess certain sins that we have committed. Yet, if we try to hide things by using deceptive language or by omitting sins, we end up feeling guilty for doing so—as well as for what we had originally done.

By being transparent with our confessor, we can experience the healing mercy of God Who is always ready to forgive us.

PRAYER. *Have mercy on me, Lord, for I am a sinner.*

WE HAVE in heaven the heart of a mother who understands our troubles and consoles us.

—St. Leopold Mandić

SEPT. 8

The Birth of Mary

REFLECTION. Today we celebrate the birth of the Blessed Virgin Mary. God intended that from the moment of her conception she be protected from sin so that she might be free to accept the invitation of the Angel to become the Mother of the Son of God.

But she also was predestined to be our own heavenly Mother as well.

PRAYER. *Hail Mary, blessed are you among women.*

MAKE frequent acts of infinite gratitude to God. —St. Paschal Baylon

SEPT. 9

Thank You, Lord

REFLECTION. When Jesus healed ten lepers, only one returned to thank the Lord. We easily can develop a sense of entitlement. We can fail to note how others are serving us. Gratitude helps to cure either shortcoming.

By saying "Thank you" often, to God and to others, we remember how graced we are. We have no time for resentment or jealousy.

PRAYER. *I thank You, O Lord, for all the wonderful ways You have graced me.*

FLEE from useless rumors, for in these things the will of man wavers.

—Bl. Giles of Assisi

SEPT. 10

Rumors and Gossip

REFLECTION. It is a sad fact that many people who belong to organizations that are dedicated to growth in the spiritual life spend too much time gossiping and spreading rumors.

We easily could be guilty of a form of murder, for we are killing another person's reputation. We should try to see what is good in the other, even if it is not readily apparent.

PRAYER. *May every word I say build up and not damage the Kingdom of God.*

TWO things the devil fears above all: the fire of charity and the well-trodden path of humility. —St. Anthony of Padua

SEPT. 11

Charity and Humility

REFLECTION. When we practice acts of charity, we sometimes do so for our own purposes (even if we do not fully realize it). We might do them to make us feel better about ourselves or to make us look good in the sight of others.

When we view our charity as an honor and a gift given to us by God, we will be practicing our charity in true humility.

PRAYER. *May I always be grateful to those whom I am called to serve.*

LOVE the Madonna and pray the Rosary, for her Rosary is the weapon against the evils of the world today.

—St. Pius of Pietrelcina

SEPT. 12

Hail Mary, Full of Grace

REFLECTION. Franciscans have always considered the Blessed Virgin Mary to be the Queen of the Franciscan Order. Her Name is precious to those who call upon her, for she is a true model and mother, guide, and friend to all who pray to her.

It is difficult to think of following Christ without making His Mother an important part of our lives.

PRAYER. *May the Name of Mary be praised throughout the whole world.*

O BLESSED poverty, which bestows eternal riches on those who love and embrace her. —St. Clare of Assisi

SEPT. 13

Queen Poverty

REFLECTION. Very few of us can live a life of the heroic embrace of poverty as witnessed by St. Francis and St. Clare. All of us are called to a life of ever greater detachment from what we own—be it physical possessions or our opinions and attitudes.

When we own nothing of our own, then we can enjoy all that God intends for us.

PRAYER. *Lord, may all I am and all I own be Yours.*

THE Cross is the school of love.

—St. Maximilian Kolbe

SEPT. 14

The Exaltation of the Cross

REFLECTION. The Gospel of John calls the Crucifixion the hour of glory. It defines the meaning of "glory" as the outpouring of love. We most clearly see how much God loves us when we gaze at the Cross: God loves us to death.

We are most like God when we are willing to carry our crosses, when we die to ourselves to die and rise with Christ.

PRAYER. *O Jesus, grant us the strength to bear our crosses as You bore the Cross.*

THE memory of the poverty felt by Christ and His Mother often reduced Francis to tears. —St. Bonaventure

SEPT. 15

Our Lady of Sorrows

REFLECTION. Mary shared the poverty of Christ; she shared in His Passion. In this, she was practicing compassion (which means "to suffer with"). St. Francis likewise shared in their pain.

Each of us is called to meditate upon their suffering, and—even more—to join our sufferings to theirs, to practice compassion in our own lives.

PRAYER. *Our Lady of Sorrows, pray for us.*

GRACE draws grace, and one vice leads to another vice. —Bl. Giles of Assisi

SEPT. 16

The Butterfly Effect

REFLECTION. One small change in the world can have an effect on other things around it, and then those things can change other things—until what began as a small action in one part of the world changes something much greater in another part of the world.

This is true both of virtue and vice. Both are contagious.

PRAYER. *May I spread goodness in this world and not vice.*

TRUE love of Christ had now transformed his lover into his image.

—St. Bonaventure

SEPT. 17

The Stigmata of St. Francis

REFLECTION. On Mount Alvernia, St. Francis was signed with the marks of the Passion of his beloved Savior. Often, when people live together for a long time—and especially if they love each other—they begin to resemble each other.

Called to rebuild the Church from the cross of San Damiano, St. Francis was becoming a living image of that cross.

PRAYER. *We adore You, O Christ, for by your Holy Cross, You have redeemed the world.*

YOU are the Spirit, and I am only the trumpet, and without Your breath I can give no sound. —St. Joseph of Cupertino

SEPT. 18

The Message of the Spirit of God

REFLECTION. Although St. Joseph of Cupertino was not gifted intellectually, when he surrendered to the Spirit of God speaking through him, he was able to share the wisdom of the mysteries of our Faith.

We are likewise called to be so filled with the Spirit that everything we say, everything we do, is imbued with the Holy Spirit.

PRAYER. *Spirit of God, descend upon me. Fill me with Your Wisdom.*

BEWARE of trying to accomplish anything by force. —St. Angela Merici

SEPT. 19

Blessed Are the Meek

REFLECTION. We might be tempted to try to change the world by force. We might even convince ourselves that we are doing this out of love.

But we are called to be like the Suffering Servant, Who responded to persecution like a gentle lamb that was led to the slaughter. Only love will change the world and the hearts of those who are sinners.

PRAYER. *Fill my heart with gentleness, Lord, for only the meek will inherit Your Kingdom.*

BEFORE everything, fidelity to the Church: One, Holy, Catholic and Apostolic. —Pope St. John XXIII

SEPT. 20

Called to Be Catholic

REFLECTION. When St. Francis founded the Franciscan Order, he sought the approval for his Movement from the Holy Father in Rome. Unlike many other reformers, he considered himself to be a faithful child of the Church.

While he was aware of the problems that existed in the Church, he did not want to criticize or destroy it—but rather he wanted to heal it with his love.

PRAYER. *I believe in One, Holy, Catholic and Apostolic Church.*

HAPPY that person whose words issue from the Holy Spirit and not from himself. —St. Anthony of Padua

SEPT. 21

The Feast of St. Matthew the Evangelist

REFLECTION. The Gospel of St. Matthew was inspired by the Holy Spirit. As at the Annunciation, the Holy Spirit combined what was Divine (the inspiration) with what was human (the talents of the human author) to produce the living Word of God.

Thus, the infallible truth of the Gospel is the faith message, and not so much the secondary details.

PRAYER. *St. Matthew, pray for us.*

TRUE progress quietly and persistently moves along without notice. —St. Francis de Sales

SEPT. 22

Not Living in the Limelight

REFLECTION. St. Joseph, the foster father of Jesus, is a wonderful example of someone who worked quietly and consistently to fulfill God's Will.

Our goal in the spiritual life is not to be well known; it is not to call attention to what we have accomplished—but it is to serve generously without any expectation of profiting from what we have done.

PRAYER. *Lord, let me never draw attention to myself or what I do.*

THE Cross will not crush you; if its weight makes you stagger, its power will also sustain you.

—St. Pius of Pietrelcina

SEPT. 23

Carrying the Cross

REFLECTION. St. Pius of Pietrelcina bore the marks of the Stigmata for most of his priestly life. Like St. Francis, Padre Pio became a living sign of the Passion of Our Lord.

We, too, are called to become sacraments (visible signs of an invisible grace) of the Passion of the Lord by the way that we respond to the crosses of our own lives.

PRAYER. *Behold the wood of the Cross, on which hung the Savior of the world.*

PLACE your labor humbly in the Lord and God will place His grace in thee.

—Bl. Giles of Assisi

SEPT. 24

Unless the Lord Builds the City

REFLECTION. It is important to remember that we are not in control—but rather God is. We are called to collaborate with God's grace so that everything we do might be done in His Name.

When we rely upon our own talents and efforts too much, we encounter frustration because things never really work out how we hope that they would.

PRAYER. *Lord, may all that I do be done in Your Name and by Your grace.*

THERE are no galley slaves in the royal vessel of divine love—every man works his oar voluntarily.

—St. Francis de Sales

SEPT. 25

We Choose to Follow

REFLECTION. Our service of the Kingdom of God is not something that He has imposed on us. Our obedience to God's Will is not some form of slavery.

We embrace both with our free will. They do not rob us of our freedom and dignity. Rather, they assist us in becoming who and what God created us to be.

PRAYER. *Lord, I freely choose to follow You. I freely want to take Your Cross upon my shoulders.*

ALWAYS without wearying, focus your attention on what is above you and let the love of God be like oil poured over everything.

—St. Paschal Baylon

SEPT. 26

Blessed Are the Pure of Heart, for They Shall See God

REFLECTION. The above Beatitude speaks of the pure of heart. The heart, in the Bible, is where one thinks. If our hearts are pure, if we think constantly about things from above, then we will be able to see God.

When we do not feel the presence of God, most often it is because we have allowed our thoughts to dwell on other things.

PRAYER. *Lord, may my first thought of the day and my last be of You.*

CHARITY has to be universal, which means we have to love everyone, because all are children of God.

—Bl. Jacques Ghazir Haddad

SEPT. 27

Charity as an Act of Love

REFLECTION. St. Vincent de Paul once said that we can only hope that the poor will forgive us our charity. Too often we serve the poor to feel good about ourselves.

When we have served others, we should thank them for having been able to share both our love and our service with them.

PRAYER. *Lord, may I see Your face in everyone whom I am called to serve.*

AN HOUR of patience is more than a day of fasting.

—St. John Bosco

SEPT. 28

There Is No Rush

REFLECTION. A lack of patience is a sign that we want to be in charge.

We have to learn to be patient with those around us (for maybe they need time), with ourselves (for maybe God has not yet given us the grace that we need to change), and especially with God (for He will act in His time and not ours).

PRAYER. *Lord, grant me serenity and patience.*

A NGELS, write this promise in the book of life: I am of Jesus and Jesus is mine.
—Bl. Veronica Antal

SEPT. 29

The Archangels

REFLECTION. The Angels of God are sent as messengers to console us or to protect us from harm. In addition, they have the task of challenging us to greater fidelity.

Michael, Gabriel, and Raphael—with the other Angels—serve God wholly and completely, and they call us to follow Him with just as much fervor as they do.

PRAYER. *Holy Angels of God, pray for us.*

A PREACHER of the Word of God is placed by God to be the light, example, and standard-bearer of the people of God.
—Bl. Giles of Assisi

SEPT. 30

Living What One Preaches

REFLECTION. There are those who preach the Word of God as official ministers of the Church. There also are those who preach in an everyday manner with words and—more importantly—with their lives.

It is essential to be consistent; that is, to live in an authentic and transparent manner the messages that we have shared with others.

PRAYER. *May the first person to whom I preach always be me.*

THE best perfection for a religious is to do common things in a perfect manner. —St. Anthony of Padua

OCT. 1

The Little Flower

REFLECTION. Although she was not a Franciscan, the spirituality of St. Thérèse of the Child Jesus is consistent with what St. Francis and St. Clare taught and lived.

She taught that very few of us have the opportunity to do great things in our lives. But all of us can do small, everyday things with great love.

PRAYER. *May I meet You, Lord, in the everyday events of my life.*

DO NOT try to please everybody. Try to please God, the Angels and the Saints. They are your public. —St. John Vianney

OCT. 2

The Feast of the Guardian Angels

REFLECTION. Guardian Angels are often portrayed as being cute and consoling, but that is not a complete picture of who they are and what they do. As messengers of God, they also call us to greater faithfulness.

The generous service that they perform for us is furthermore an example of how we should be ready to serve others.

PRAYER. *My Guardian Angel, protect me and guide me to the Lord.*

BE AS blind to the faults of your neighbor as possible, trying at least to attribute a good intention to their actions.

—Bl. Solanus Casey

OCT. 3

Not Judging Others' Actions

REFLECTION. While it is perfectly acceptable to judge the conduct of others, it is not a good thing to judge their motivations. We often do not know what has prompted their actions. We also may be unaware of their strengths and weaknesses.

Rather than being a harsh judge of their actions, we should try to offer the most positive explanation possible for their behavior.

PRAYER. *May I be as compassionate a judge of others' actions as I pray that You will be of mine.*

LET us begin, brothers, to serve the Lord God, for up to now we have made little or no progress.

—St. Francis of Assisi

OCT. 4

A Constant Conversion

REFLECTION. For as much as St. Francis gave an incredible example of love and devotion, he always felt that he and his brothers were called to give more and more.

Each day is a day for a deeper conversion of our hearts. We do the best we can today, and tomorrow we try to do just a bit more.

PRAYER. *My Lord and my God, my God and my All.*

WHEN the fire of love is ablaze, it cannot be constrained within the heart, but blazes forth and burns, consumes and absorbs other hearts.

OCT. 5

—St. Maximilian Kolbe

Holiness Is Contagious

REFLECTION. One of the best ways to call others to conversion is to live our own faith life well. Words are cheap. Guilt and fear do not bring people to true conversion.

But if people see us on fire with love for the Lord and truly joyful in our devotion, then they will want to have what we have found.

PRAYER. *Inflame my heart with Your love, O Lord, and let my example inflame the hearts of others as well.*

ST. FRANCIS burned with love for the Sacrament of our Lord's Body with all his heart, and was lost in wonder of such condescending love.

OCT. 6

—St. Bonaventure

St. Francis and the Eucharist

REFLECTION. St. Francis marveled at how Jesus was born as a child in Bethlehem. How could God descend to our condition and become one of us?

Yet, this also is what He does when the bread and wine of the Eucharist become His Body and Blood. Jesus is made present again to us physically, and we are invited to become one with Him.

PRAYER. *May I always honor the Sacrament of Your Body and Blood, Lord Jesus.*

LET us go, my Brother, with rosary in hand, our eyes to the ground, and our spirit in heaven. —St. Felix of Cantalice

OCT. 7

Our Lady of the Rosary

REFLECTION. The recitation of the Rosary gives us time to reflect on the great mysteries of the life of Christ and His Blessed Mother.

The prayers of the Rosary—the Our Father, Hail Mary, and Glory Be—serve as a background for our meditation on God acting in the lives of Jesus and Mary, as well as on how He continues to act in our lives today.

PRAYER. *Blessed are you among women, and blessed is the fruit of your womb, Jesus.*

I DO not want to go it on my own, for by myself I would not know how to want, desire or seek it. —St. Angela of Foligno

OCT. 8

Depending on the Lord

REFLECTION. Jesus invited us to put His yoke upon ourselves. Ancient yokes were intended for two animals. We cannot plow the furrow alone because then it would lean off to one side. We need to do this together with Him.

Furthermore, since He is Wisdom itself, we have to allow Him to lead the way, for on our own we will get lost.

PRAYER. *Lord, lead me, guide me, teach me Your ways.*

IN THE spiritual life, he who does not advance goes backwards.

—St. Pius of Pietrelcina

OCT. 9

Ongoing Conversion

REFLECTION. Our commitment to the Lord is not a choice made once and for all. It has to be renewed each day—as well as in each and every event of our daily lives.

Consider how we bless ourselves with holy water every time we enter a church. This action is a renewal of our baptismal commitment.

PRAYER. *I am Yours, O Lord, today and each and every day of my life.*

IN ALL your endeavors have a good intention; do everything for God without being influenced by human respect.

—Bl. Angela Truszkowska

OCT. 10

Purifying Our Motives

REFLECTION. It is easy to do things with mixed motivations. While we think we are doing things completely for the Lord, we often have hidden motives that are more concerned with our own needs.

It is when we are challenged or even rejected—and continue doing the right things—that we can be sure we are doing them out of love for the Lord.

PRAYER. *Lord, may all that I think, may all that I do, be an expression of my love for You.*

CONSULT not your fears but your hopes and dreams. Think not about your frustrations, but about your unfulfilled potential. —Pope St. John XXIII

OCT. 11

Hopes and Dreams

REFLECTION. If we concentrate on what is wrong with this world, then we will become negative and frustrated. If, however, we concentrate on the good, both what exists and what could come to be, then we will be filled with a sense of hope.

This is not to ignore the problems around us, but rather not to let them control who we are.

PRAYER. *Lord, teach the young to have their visions and the elderly to dream their dreams.*

TRULY, matters in the world are in a bad state; but if you and I begin in earnest to reform ourselves, a really good beginning will have been made.

—St. Peter of Alcantara

OCT. 12

I Can Convert Myself Alone

REFLECTION. We easily can become discouraged when we see some of the bad happenings in the world.

Rather than letting this paralyze us, however, we can choose to dedicate ourselves to our own conversion. In turn, this can serve as an invitation to others to do the same. In this way—one heart at a time—we will transform the world.

PRAYER. *Grant me the grace to seek You more and to reject everything that is not of You.*

WOE to the religious who amuses himself with silly gossip, trying to make people laugh.

—St. Francis of Assisi

OCT. 13

The Danger of Gossip

REFLECTION. How do we know if what we are saying about another is gossip? A good rule of thumb is to ask ourselves, "Is it true? Is it kind? Is it helpful?"

If we cannot say "Yes" to all of these questions, then what we are sharing is probably gossip—and we should not be involved in spreading it.

PRAYER. *Lord, may what I say always be true, kind, and helpful.*

IF A man had lived from Adam even till the end of the world, and had done all the good he could, he would not merit the least condescension from God. **—Bl. Giles of Assisi**

OCT. 14

It Is All Gift

REFLECTION. At times, we can begin to think that we are earning God's love through our good deeds. But God already loves us more than we could ever embrace or even comprehend.

What changes when we do good deeds is not God's attitude toward us, but rather our ability to accept God's free gift of grace.

PRAYER. *I thank You, O Lord, for Your gifts of grace and love.*

WHEN a person is enkindled with divine fire, he becomes totally inflamed, totally ablaze and melting with the love of God. **OCT. 15**

—St. Anthony of Padua

The Divine Fire of God's Love

REFLECTION. St. Teresa of Avila warned against seeking extraordinary spiritual experiences such as ecstasies or visions or locutions.

We express our love for God most often in the everyday experiences of life. Our choice is to show God our love by our devotion, our integrity, and our fidelity to what we promised to be.

PRAYER. *Inflame my heart with Your love, O Lord, and may that flame never be extinguished.*

THE Most Sacred Heart of Jesus is the love of God toward mankind. **OCT. 16**

—St. Maximilian Kolbe

The Revelations of the Sacred Heart

REFLECTION. In the 17th century, St. Margaret Mary Alacoque received the revelations of the Sacred Heart of Jesus.

Like the devotion to Divine Mercy, which is widespread in these times, devotion to the Sacred Heart was and is a celebration of the incredible love and mercy that Jesus showed us in His Death upon the Cross—and continues to show us each day of our lives.

PRAYER. *Sacred Heart of Jesus, have mercy on me.*

IT IS not enough to carry the Cross in order to be saved. It is essential to carry it with Christ, and like Christ.

—St. Ignatius of Santhiá

OCT. 17

St. Ignatius of Antioch

REFLECTION. St. Ignatius of Antioch was called to his cross, martyrdom in Rome, late in his life. But even on the way to his own death, he exercised his ministry by writing a series of letters to various communities.

He did not get caught up in his own difficulties, but rather used even his forthcoming death as a lesson in the Faith.

PRAYER. *May I be like wheat that is ground up to make the pure Bread of Christ.*

LOVING compassion made him regard everything with affection but especially the souls which Jesus Christ redeemed with His precious Blood. —St. Bonaventure

OCT. 18

Loving the Redeemed of the Lord

REFLECTION. God created every person in His image and likeness. The Blood of Christ on the Cross redeemed every person.

Given the incredible dignity with which each of us is endowed and the terrible price of our redemption, how could we not view each and every person with great affection? Each one is extremely precious to the Lord.

PRAYER. *Lord, may I always treat each person I meet with the same dignity I would show You.*

DO NOT believe that everything is lost when things do not go according to your expectations. —Bl. Veronica Antal

OCT. 19

The Jesuit Martyrs

REFLECTION. Many of the Jesuits who traveled to the New World to evangelize the Native Americans were drawn by a sense of duty, but the mission eventually became one of love.

It did not proceed in the way that they had hoped. They witnessed death and disease and continual setbacks, but by dying for the Faith, they preached the Gospel in flesh and blood.

PRAYER. *May I be willing to pay any price to proclaim the Gospel in word and deed.*

CHARITY is that with which no man is lost and without which no man is saved. —St. Charles Borromeo

OCT. 20

The Importance of Charity

REFLECTION. Our faith cannot be only an internal affirmation of our beliefs; it also must express itself in how we reach out to others.

Our charity leads us to salvation not because God will save us as a reward for having done good deeds. Rather, in serving others, we already are living in God's love.

PRAYER. *Lord, may I always see my service to others as an opportunity to love them as You love them.*

OUR will must always be dependent on Him, which is why we pray, "Thy will be done." —St. Braulio of Saragossa

OCT. 21

Surrender to God's Plan

REFLECTION. We all try to take care of ourselves, and many of us dread the idea that one day we will be reliant on others. Yet, we always are truly dependent, for God calls us to surrender to His Will each day of our lives.

If we do this in small, everyday ways, it will be easier to face the ultimate surrender.

PRAYER. *Not my will, but Your Will be done.*

THE trouble is that everyone talks about reforming others and no one thinks about reforming himself. —St. Peter of Alcantara

OCT. 22

Being Honest with Ourselves

REFLECTION. It is so easy to see the flaws in everyone around us, but so difficult to admit that we share many of those same attitudes and behaviors.

We have to learn to find the humility and profound honesty to judge ourselves rightly. We have to learn to find the patience and compassion to judge others' actions as we would hope they would judge ours.

PRAYER. *May I take the plank out of my own eye, O Lord, before I try to take the splinter out of the eye of another.*

GLOW with the brightness that comes from the good example of a praiseworthy and blameless life.

—St. John of Capistrano

OCT. 23

Giving Good Witness

REFLECTION. If others could see everything that we do, if they could read the most secret thoughts of our hearts, would they be edified or scandalized? The goal in the spiritual life is to be people of integrity.

We want to be transparent so that there are no secrets, no inconsistencies between what we are called to be and what we actually are.

PRAYER. *Lord, may I always truly be what I say that I am.*

YOU are rewarded not according to your work or your time but according to the measure of your love.

—St. Bernardine of Siena

OCT. 24

It Is the Effort That Matters

REFLECTION. All of us have not received the same talents. We do not have the same challenges. It is important not to judge our efforts by an external evaluation that does not take into account what God expects of us.

God wants us to try our best, so that we love as much as is possible in our particular situation.

PRAYER. *May I always try my best, O Lord, and not be disappointed when things do not work out as I would have wished.*

THE most deadly poison of our times is indifference. —St. Maximilian Kolbe

OCT. 25

Not Being Lukewarm

REFLECTION. Elie Wiesel said that the opposite of love is not hate—it is indifference. We have to be concerned with what is happening in the world.

Likewise, we cannot be indifferent to the state of our spiritual life. While we want to avoid becoming obsessive, we still have to work at correcting our flaws, whatever they might be.

PRAYER. *Lord, may I never be lukewarm and indifferent.*

HUMILITY and purity are the wings which carry us to God and make us almost divine. —St. Pius of Pietrelcina

OCT. 26

Emptying Our Hearts of What Is Not from God

REFLECTION. When we are filled with pride, we act as if we were our own god. When we act with impurity, we are worshiping our passions as if they were gods.

Humility and purity open our hearts to be filled with the goodness of God. They also allow us to be truly available and compassionate to those around us.

PRAYER. *Humble my spirit, O Lord, and purify my desires.*

GOD is really present in the consecrated Host as He is in the glory of Heaven.
—St. Paschal Baylon

OCT. 27

Devotion to the Eucharist

REFLECTION. Devotion to the Eucharist—whether it be at Holy Mass or Eucharistic Adoration or during a simple visit to a church to kneel or sit in front of the Eucharist—has always been a central aspect of Franciscan devotion.

Franciscans never considered the Eucharist as something to do, but rather It is Someone to meet.

PRAYER. *Soul of Christ, sanctify me. Body of Christ, save me.*

HE WAS armed with the Cross, the means of salvation which would enable him to escape from a shipwrecked world.
—St. Bonaventure

OCT. 28

The Cross, the Means of Our Salvation

REFLECTION. Origen, a Father of the Church, spoke of how the wood of the Cross actually came from the wood that Noah had used to build the ark during the flood.

The wood that saved Noah and his family in turn saved all of us from the flood of lies and hurt and sin that drown the goodness and love with which God created the world.

PRAYER. *May I always honor the wood of the Cross on which my Savior hung.*

WHERE there is quiet and meditation, there is neither preoccupation nor dissipation.

—St. Francis of Assisi

OCT. 29

Finding God's Peace

REFLECTION. We cannot expect to find the peace of the Lord if we are constantly surrounded by noise and activity.

We need to slow down and turn off some of our devices and spend time in silent meditation and prayer. We should do this for a short time each day, but we also should plan weekend or longer retreats.

PRAYER. *Silence my heart and my surroundings, O Lord, so that I might hear Your voice.*

O LORD, extend Your hands which were nailed to the Cross, to give us a gift. Whatever You touch will be cleansed and healed.

—St. Anthony of Padua

OCT. 30

The Wounds of Our Healing

REFLECTION. Jesus wants us to know that He loves us, that He forgives us. He thus permitted Himself to be tortured and nailed to the Cross.

His arms were stretched out in a way that forever unites heaven and earth, and in a way that shows that He is waiting to hold us in His loving embrace.

PRAYER. *May I die to myself out of love for You Who were nailed to the Cross out of love for me.*

BEWARE of talkativeness because he that uses many words hurts his soul. **OCT. 31**

—Bl. Giles of Assisi

Know How to Speak Prudently

REFLECTION. Silence and solitude are most lacking in our busy, noisy world. We only add to that clamor when we fill our days with useless chatter.

Speaking less, listening more, and preserving silence can be of enormous assistance in our spiritual quest. We need to be able to hear ourselves, and—most of all—we need to be able to hear God.

PRAYER. *Speak to me, O Lord, in the quiet of my heart.*

THE Saints and their remembrance were for St. Francis like a burning coal, which enkindled in him a divine fire. **NOV. 1**

—St. Bonaventure

All Saints' Day

REFLECTION. St. Francis loved the Saints and their memory, but he warned his followers not to presume upon their own holiness. God calls each of us to become a Saint.

We have to reflect the light and the heat of the divine fire upon a world that has become all too dark and cold. May the Saints in heaven help and guide us in this endeavor.

PRAYER. *Saints of the Lord, bless the Lord!*

WE MUST empty Purgatory with our prayers. —St. Pius of Pietrelcina

NOV. 2

Praying for Our Beloved Deceased

REFLECTION. Purgatory is that state in which the deceased are asked to surrender every brokenness and selfishness they still have.

We pray for people in Purgatory because our prayers are a form of love—and it is easier for them to choose eternal love if they themselves are being loved. It could be said that we're loving them into heaven.

PRAYER. *Eternal rest grant unto them, O Lord, and let perpetual light shine upon them.*

CHRIST'S wounds are all we need to study. —St. Bernard of Corleone

NOV. 3

Meditating on the Passion of Christ

REFLECTION. When we meditate on how much God loves us—literally to death—we realize that we are precious in His eyes. Therefore, it is good to consider the Passion and Death of Jesus.

Praying the Way of the Cross, gazing upon the wounds of Christ in meditation, and reading the Passion Narratives in the Gospels are all useful examples of how we can do this.

PRAYER. *Lord Jesus, may Your Cross always help me to recall Your love.*

IF WE wish to make any progress in the service of God we must begin every day with new eagerness. —St. Charles Borromeo

NOV. 4

Renewing Our Enthusiasm Each Day

REFLECTION. It is easy to get into a rut and to do things simply because they are expected of us. It is essential to make a conscious choice—each day—of what we are going to do.

Furthermore, the goal would be to choose those things with enthusiasm because it is through them that we can express our love for God and others.

PRAYER. *Renew my spirit each day, O Lord, so that I might embrace the tasks of my life with joy.*

IF THE devil can call his own even one hair of a man's head, he will lose no time in making a rope of it. —St. Bonaventure

NOV. 5

The Cleverness of the Devil

REFLECTION. The devil rarely asks us to do truly horrific, terrible things. The devil tends to work in a more subtle manner, tempting us to compromise in small ways, a little at a time.

But it is a slippery slope. One small sin leads to another greater sin; one white lie leads to a lie of a darker hue; a little festering resentment leads to lasting hate.

PRAYER. *St. Michael, protect me from the wiles of the devil.*

S**EE everything, overlook a great deal, correct a little.** —Pope St. John XXIII

NOV. 6

Recognizing What Is Truly Important

REFLECTION. If we constantly are correcting others, we probably are not doing so for their good—but rather we are expressing our own perfectionism.

We should keep our eyes open to what is going on, but we don't have to try to fix everything or everyone right away. It often is wise to allow people to recognize the need to change on their own.

PRAYER. *Lord, teach me when to speak and when to hold my tongue.*

W**HAT is deferred is not avoided.** —St. Thomas More

NOV. 7

Procrastination

REFLECTION. There always is a tendency to put off things, especially if they are not our favorite things to do. If we have taken on a responsibility, however, we have an obligation to fulfill it because it is being done not only for us, but also for others.

The importance of not putting off things is true especially when it refers to our prayer time and spiritual reading.

PRAYER. *May I do now, O Lord, what needs to be done.*

CHRIST wears two shoes in the world: Scripture and nature.

—Bl. John Duns Scotus

NOV. 8

Meeting Christ in Word and Deed

REFLECTION. Scripture is the Word of God, and it is essential to read and study it to come to know Who God is and what He wants of us.

Nature bears the fingerprints of God. By celebrating the marvels of creation, we are filled with awe at the goodness of God Who saw that everything He made was good.

PRAYER. *Lord God, may I hear You in Your Word; may I see You in what You have created.*

WE SHOULD visit churches often and show great reverence for the clergy.

—St. Francis of Assisi

NOV. 9

The Dedication of St. John Lateran

REFLECTION. Today we celebrate the dedication of the Basilica that St. Francis entered when he visited the Holy Father to receive his approval for the Franciscan way of life.

St. Francis often spoke of how we should visit churches frequently to pay reverence to the Eucharistic Lord and the enthroned Word of God in the Sacred Scriptures.

PRAYER. *We praise the Lord Who is present in all the churches throughout the whole world.*

PRAYER fills people with light, strength, and consolation. —St. Rose of Viterbo

NOV. 10

Prayer, the Source of Our Peace

REFLECTION. While we pray to God and for others, our prayer nevertheless also changes our own hearts.

When we pray, we learn to surrender to the Providence and Will of God. We spend time with Someone Whom we love. We remember that He always is there for us. We find the strength to do what we should do.

PRAYER. *Lord, please meet me in my prayer so that You and I might be one.*

LET your words be few and useful and thoughtful. —Bl. Giles of Assisi

NOV. 11

Words Can Help—and They Can Hurt

REFLECTION. Words can have a powerful effect upon the world. St. James speaks of them as being like a spark in a dry forest or the rudder on a ship. They can change everything.

We therefore should choose our words with care and use them to build up the Kingdom. Furthermore, at times our best response to a situation is silent prayer.

PRAYER. *May all my words be filled with Your Spirit and Life.*

THE purpose of creation, the purpose of man is to become more and more like the Creator. —St. Maximilian Kolbe

NOV. 12

To Become like God

REFLECTION. God created human beings in His image and likeness. By our selfishness and sinfulness, we have obscured that dignity. God calls us to return to the original purpose for which He created us.

We need to root out from ourselves anything that is not of God and fill that void with His love alone.

PRAYER. *May I put on Christ so that I resemble Him in all my being.*

DISORDER in society is the result of disorder in the family. —St. Angela Merici

NOV. 13

Caring for Our Families

REFLECTION. There is a tendency among some who are dedicated to service in the Church to spend large amounts of time in their apostolate at the cost of not spending enough time with their own families.

Pope St. Paul VI spoke of how the family is the first church that most people attend. It is there that we have to offer our greatest care.

PRAYER. *Mary, Joseph, teach me how I should treat my own family.*

LET us trust in God, then, but trust Him without limits. —St. Maximilian Kolbe

NOV. 14

Trusting without Limits

REFLECTION. For as much as we try to have faith in the Lord, there are times when we give to God with one hand and take back with the other. The father of a son possessed by a demon in the Gospel of Mark says, "I do believe. Help my unbelief."

As much as possible, we have to surrender our doubts and hesitancy and place our trust entirely in the Lord.

PRAYER. *Lord, You are my Rock, You are my Fortress, You are my All.*

JUST as food is necessary to the life of the body, so good reading is necessary to the life of the soul. —Pope St. John XXIII

NOV. 15

Spiritual Reading

REFLECTION. One of the first things that most people abandon when they get busy is spiritual reading. This is dangerous, for we are constantly invited and encouraged to read more and more information.

We need to make sure that at least some of what we read is spiritual in nature. We need reminders of who we are and what we want to become.

PRAYER. *Lord, help me to find those books that will best lead me to You.*

EVERY Christian must be a living book wherein one can read the teachings of the Gospels. —St. Joseph of Leonissa

NOV. 16

A Saint on Sunday, a Devil on Monday

REFLECTION. Many people will never read the Bible or even religious pamphlets. The only Gospel that they will see is the way in which we live our lives.

Our behavior should be so transparent that people see in our actions the values by which we live. On the other hand, people should never be scandalized by seeing us do something that contradicts our values.

PRAYER. *Lord, teach me to be consistent in the witness I give by my life.*

HOW could I bear a crown of gold when the Lord bears a crown of thorns? And bears it for me! —St. Elizabeth of Hungary

NOV. 17

Jesus, the King of Kings

REFLECTION. St. Elizabeth of Hungary, a queen, gave up her honors to serve the poor and the sick. She followed Jesus' example: He was a King Whose crown was not made of gold but rather of thorns; His throne was not one of majesty but rather one of the wood of the Cross.

This is the glory to which we, too, are called.

PRAYER. *Lord Jesus, You are the King of my life, the King of my heart.*

LET all the brothers be Catholics, and live and speak in a Catholic manner.

—St. Francis of Assisi

NOV. 18

The Dedication of the Basilicas of Peter and Paul

REFLECTION. Today we commemorate the dedication of the Basilicas of the two pillars of the Faith: Sts. Peter and Paul. Franciscan spirituality is always united with the Church.

St. Francis wanted to reform the Church. He, in fact, saw his role as rebuilding it. Yet, he wanted to do this not with criticism and anger, but rather with love and by his own example.

PRAYER. *Sts. Peter and Paul, pray for us.*

WHAT a great laudable exchange: to leave the things of time for those of eternity, to choose the things of heaven for the goods of earth.

—St. Clare of Assisi

NOV. 19

The Things That Are Above

REFLECTION. While St. Agnes of Assisi chose those things that are above by living in the cloister of the Poor Clares, we are called to make choices each day that are based either upon earthly considerations or heavenly things.

To choose heavenly things does not mean to run away from our everyday lives, but rather to consecrate them in God's grace.

PRAYER. *May all I do be done in Your Name and Your love, O Lord.*

LOVE'S object is two-fold: God and neighbor. In reality there is one single object: God and His image.

—Bl. Jacques Ghazir Haddad

NOV. 20

Vertical and Horizontal

REFLECTION. Throughout salvation history, people of faith have realized that they are called to love God (the vertical dimension of our faith) and love their neighbor (the horizontal dimension of our faith). Jesus Himself taught that these are the greatest of all commandments.

Without God, our faith is social work; without neighbor, our faith is an empty theory.

PRAYER. *May I love the Lord with heart, soul, mind, and strength, and my neighbor as myself.*

OH, MY sweet queen, from now on I don't want anyone to exceed me in love for you. —Bl. Veronica Antal

NOV. 21

The Presentation of Mary

REFLECTION. It is appropriate to celebrate the day when Sts. Joachim and Anne brought the child Mary to present her to the Lord in the Temple.

In the Gospel of Luke, in fact, we see that Mary is presented as the new Ark of the Covenant, for it was through her that Jesus became manifest in the world.

PRAYER. *Blessed Virgin Mary, Ark of the Covenant, pray for us.*

IT IS always springtime in the heart that loves God. —St. John Vianney

NOV. 22

The Soul in Love

REFLECTION. The Song of Songs speaks about how spring arrives for the Lover and Beloved. Over the centuries, this canticle has been applied to how we are called to fall in love with the Lord.

Our faith is not a question of keeping rules or performing penitential practices. It is rather a willingness to abandon ourselves to the Other, to make the Other the center of our reality.

PRAYER. *Lord, I love You, I love You, I love You.*

THE root of all evil is "I," "Me," and "Mine." —St. Pius of Pietrelcina

NOV. 23

The Danger of the Ego

REFLECTION. Jesus taught His disciples that we have to love others as we love ourselves. But thinking about myself all the time is not true love of self.

If I truly loved myself, then I would challenge myself to reach out and serve others, for true love is a willingness to forget one's own wants in order to serve others' needs.

PRAYER. *Root out my selfishness from my heart, O Lord, so that I might live for You and others.*

BE HUMBLE in such a way that your patience is the proof of your humility.

—St. Bonaventure

NOV. 24

God's Time, Not Ours

REFLECTION. Patience recognizes that everything that happens in the spiritual life happens in God's time rather than our own. Patience understands that God is in control and we are not.

We are called to be patient with others (as patient as we would like God to be with us) and even patient with ourselves (for we often want to be perfect immediately).

PRAYER. *Lord, may I patiently await Your time, and not insist upon my own plan.*

IT IS because of faith that we exchange the present for the future.

—St. Fidelis of Sigmaringen

NOV. 25

Trusting in the Future That God Has Promised Us

REFLECTION. The early Martyrs of the Church, like St. Catherine of Alexandria, had to trust that God would not abandon them even as they faced martyrdom. We, too, are called upon in big ways and small to give witness to our faith, even if doing so will cost us.

We trust that the joys of the present are as nothing when compared to the glory of the future.

PRAYER. *Lord, keep my eyes on the goal.*

AVOID sloth, bad company, dangerous conversations, and gambling games, remembering that time passes and never returns. —St. Leonard of Port Maurice

NOV. 26

Living Lives of Virtue

REFLECTION. While it is good to take some time off, we easily can allow that period to become a time of inappropriate distraction and conduct unbecoming of someone who is dedicated to the ways of the Lord.

We have to remember that every choice has its consequences. We are called to live our faith, even when we are relaxing.

PRAYER. *Lord, may my work, may my rest be lived in the Lord.*

I WAS indulgent [in mercy], I don't deny it; but it was You who taught me to be so. —St. Francis Anthony Fasani

NOV. 27

The Lord of Mercy

REFLECTION. The above-cited words from St. Francis Anthony Fasani are what he wanted to say to Jesus concerning his priestly ministry, especially his time in the confessional. He experienced Jesus as all merciful, and he wanted to share that mercy with all those he met.

This also would be a laudable goal for each of us—to be signs of the mercy of God.

PRAYER. *Have mercy on me, O Lord, and teach me to share that mercy with others.*

NOV. 28

BELOVED and most holy Word of God! You enlighten the hearts of the faithful, you satisfy the hungry, console the afflicted. —St. James of the Marches

God's Word

REFLECTION. The Word of God is both Jesus and the Sacred Scriptures. Jesus proclaims Who God is and what He wants of us. The Sacred Scriptures speak of God's relationship with His Holy People and teach us how we can be faithful to Jesus' call.

God speaks His Holy Word to us, and we must listen and believe and live what we have heard.

PRAYER. *Speak, Lord, for Your servant is listening.*

NOV. 29

PRAYER then, humble, trusting and loving prayer, gives light to the intellect and gives strength to the will. —St. Maximilian Kolbe

Humble Prayer

REFLECTION. The difference between magic and prayer is that in magic we say words and perform actions to control others, while in prayer we surrender to the Will of God.

Certainly, we ask for things, but we do so with the understanding that God will give us the most loving response possible. Sometimes God grants what we ask; other times His answer is "No."

PRAYER. *Listen to my prayer, O Lord, and grant what is best for me.*

BEING the servant of all, I am bound to serve all and to administer the balm-bearing words of my Lord. **NOV. 30**

—St. Francis of Assisi

Andrew, the Apostle

REFLECTION. Jesus entrusted the Apostles with His mission to proclaim the dawning of the Kingdom of God. Their proclamation was most of all the message that God had forgiven our sins and that people were called to live in His compassion.

These words were truly balm, for they were the only ones that could heal the deepest wounds of our hearts.

PRAYER. *Heal my heart and soul, O Lord, with Your balm-bearing words.*

COME, let us give a little time to folly...and even in a melancholy day let us find time for an hour of pleasure. **DEC. 1**

—St. Bonaventure

Laughing with God

REFLECTION. We don't have to be overly gloomy in the spiritual life. Rejoicing and having fun are forms of proclaiming the goodness of our Lord.

When God looked at the world He created, He found it to be very good. We almost can imagine God being not unlike a child filled with joy and wonder at finding presents under the tree on Christmas morning.

PRAYER. *Let me rejoice in You, O Lord, and in the wonders of Your creation.*

EVERYTHING should be done in light of the Kingdom of God. Our entire motivation must be centered on it. —St. Anthony of Padua

DEC. 2

Serving the Kingdom of God

REFLECTION. It is important to examine carefully the motivations for our actions. We often can do things, thinking we are doing them for the right reasons—and only later discover that we had hidden motives even unbeknown to us.

The proclamation of the Kingdom of God should be at the center of everything we think and do.

PRAYER. *May all I say and all I do proclaim the dawning of the Kingdom of God.*

HOLY contrition, holy humility, holy charity, holy devotion and holy joy make the soul holy and good.

—Bl. Giles of Assisi

DEC. 3

How to Be Holy

REFLECTION. While holiness is something that is quite unique to each person, nevertheless there are spiritual attitudes and practices that one would expect from a person seeking holiness.

Contrition for sin, humility as a recognition of one's limitations, charity as an external way to express one's faith, devotion to fostering one's rapport with Jesus and the Saints, and joy are all needed.

PRAYER. *Lord, make my soul holy and good.*

TRY to realize the dignity God has conferred on you. —St. Francis of Assisi

DEC. 4

God Thinks So Highly of Us

REFLECTION. One of the things that brings us to conversion is guilt for the ways that we have fallen short. Another is the realization that God has created us and redeemed us so that we might live with dignity as His children.

God sees all the potential that we have, and He wants us to live up to it.

PRAYER. *God, help me to see myself with the respect with which You see me.*

CHRIST'S Cross was their book, and they studied it day and night.

—St. Bonaventure

DEC. 5

Contemplate the Passion

REFLECTION. While some people read great and important books to learn about the Faith, others focus their attention on the mystery of the Cross.

When we realize how much God loved us by having His Son die in such a humble way, then we have begun to understand this great mystery of our Faith. It is not that studies are bad, but they should be subordinated to faith and prayer.

PRAYER. *Let me gaze upon Your Cross, Lord Jesus, so that I may always realize the love to which You have called me.*

IT IS a thousand times better that man should teach himself than teach the whole world. —Bl. Giles of Assisi

DEC. 6

Preaching to Ourselves

REFLECTION. It is easy to decide what everyone else should hear and do. It is much more difficult to preach to ourselves. This is especially true because most of us can rationalize what we are thinking and doing.

The first step in our own conversion is absolute, brutal honesty concerning our motivations. We must preach to ourselves first.

PRAYER. *Lord, let me hear Your call to conversion, and let me answer the call with my whole being.*

IN BOOKS we seek God; in prayer we find him. Prayer is the key which opens God's heart. —St. Pius of Pietrelcina

DEC. 7

Finding the Lord with Our Heart

REFLECTION. It is important that we learn about the things of the Lord. This helps us to love Him with our whole heart as Jesus taught in the Great Commandment.

But even more importantly, we must express our love for the Lord in prayer. In our prayer we open our heart to His Heart and they become one.

PRAYER. *May Your Holy Spirit teach me how to pray and for what I should pray.*

HE COULD do it, it was fitting, and He did it. —Bl. John Duns Scotus

DEC. 8

The Immaculate Conception

REFLECTION. There is relatively little information contained in Sacred Scripture that supports the dogma of the Immaculate Conception, and many theologians argued against it.

Bl. John Duns Scotus developed the philosophical argument that would be the basis for the declaration of that dogma: Mary was protected from sin and its effects from the moment of her conception.

PRAYER. *Remember, O Immaculate Mary, those who seek your protection and intercession.*

O NAME of Mary! Joy in the heart, honey in the mouth, melody to the ear of Her devout clients. —St. Anthony of Padua

DEC. 9

St. Juan Diego

REFLECTION. Just as St. Juan Diego encountered Mary under the title of Our Lady of Guadalupe, so now we ask her to guide us and protect us and—when necessary—challenge us.

May her Name be sweet in our mouths, and the comfort and compassion she offers those who have recourse to her be profound.

PRAYER. *Blessed be the Holy Name of Mary, Virgin and Mother.*

HOLY Spirit, beloved of the Father and Son, inflame my heart and purify my soul. —St. Paschal Baylon

DEC. 10

The Fire of the Holy Spirit

REFLECTION. As the Holy Spirit united the divine with the human in the womb of the Blessed Virgin Mary, so also the Holy Spirit inspires, purifies, and fortifies us so that we, too, might make Jesus present in this world.

We must pray for the outpouring of that Spirit upon us in this holy season of Advent.

PRAYER. *Come, Holy Spirit, fill the hearts of Your faithful.*

LET us waste no time, for life is calling, salvation is waiting, tribulation spurs us on to reach that place of rest, the abode of eternal joy. —St. Felix of Nicosia

DEC. 11

No Time to Waste

REFLECTION. It is easy to begin to drift in our lives, including in our spiritual lives. This is why tribulation, which at first seems to be totally negative, can actually end up being positive—for it forces us out of our complacency.

The Israelites needed Pharaoh's troops behind them to force them into the unknown of the desert during the Exodus.

PRAYER. *May I use today to surrender my soul to You, O Lord.*

I ASK our Lady for graces, and she immediately enfolds me in the Will of God.

—St. Veronica Giuliani

DEC. 12

Our Lady of Guadalupe

REFLECTION. Our Holy Lady has been a source of grace for Christians throughout the world. She is often invoked under many different titles, but she is the source of the same grace.

Her greatest task is to call us to faithfulness, for she wants us to surrender to God's Will in our lives—even as she did in her own life.

PRAYER. *Our Lady of Guadalupe, pray for us.*

OUR Lord sends the crosses; we do not have to invent them.

—St. Pius of Pietrelcina

DEC. 13

Accepting the Crosses of Our Lives

REFLECTION. Some people complicate their spiritual lives, inventing all sorts of penances and disciplines so that they can be more faithful to the Lord. Padre Pio reminds us that we already have difficulties and frustrations in our lives without seeking new ones.

The best approach we can take is to embrace the crosses that God has already given us.

PRAYER. *Lord, may I embrace the crosses of my life and carry them lovingly.*

BE MEEK, peaceful, and modest, courteous and humble, speaking honorably to everyone. —St. Francis of Assisi

DEC. 14

How to Conduct Ourselves in the World

REFLECTION. St. Francis admonishes us to treat everyone we meet with an exaggerated respect—to the point of treating them almost as if they were Saints.

If they are truly Saints in the eyes of God, then this is what they deserve. If they are not Saints, maybe treating them this way will make them want to become Saints.

PRAYER. *May I treat everyone I meet with the respect I would treat You, Lord.*

IF WE do this faithfully and zealously, we will experience the truth of St. Francis who says that love lightens all difficulties and sweetens all bitterness.

—Bl. Mary Frances Schervier

DEC. 15

The Source of True Joy

REFLECTION. The source of our joy is not found in the fact that we have been successful in what we have done. Our joy is found in doing what we are called to do with fidelity and enthusiasm.

We trust that God will carry all that we do to completion, but in His time and in the way that He wills.

PRAYER. *Lord, I place all I am, all that I do, into Your hands.*

THE best perfection of a religious is to do common things in a perfect manner. —St. Bonaventure

DEC. 16

We Do Not Have to Do Great Things

REFLECTION. Many of us wait for that one great event when we will meet the Lord in a powerful way. This can be futile, for most of us meet God in the everyday events of our lives.

If we apply our talents and our love to what we are doing, then we already have consecrated these things in God's grace.

PRAYER. *Lord, may I see You in the small things of life.*

BLESSED is he who is not satiated with those things which he ought always desire. —Bl. Giles of Assisi

DEC. 17

Wanting More

REFLECTION. While we should be satisfied with our proper share of the good things of the earth, we should never be satiated with God's spiritual gifts. We always should want more and more of these gifts.

This is true not because we want to accumulate them, but rather because they lead us to a greater surrender to God's love.

PRAYER. *Lord, grant that I might grow more and more in Your life and Your love.*

DEC. 18

MY EYES I have filled with Jesus upon Whom I have fixed them at the elevation of the Host at Holy Mass and I do not wish to replace Him with any other image. —St. Colette

Contemplating Christ in the Eucharist

REFLECTION. One of the most common of Franciscan devotions is contemplating before the Blessed Sacrament in Eucharistic Adoration. St. Francis marveled at the fact that God would become present in the flesh in Bethlehem—and again would become flesh upon our altars.

What a privilege to be able to spend quiet time alone with our Lord.

PRAYER. *I thank You, Lord, for Your presence in the Blessed Sacrament. I praise You.*

DEC. 19

THOSE who pray from the heart do not think about the prayer they are saying but about the God to whom they pray. —St. Francis de Sales

The True Intention of Praying

REFLECTION. Prayer is not a question of getting the words right or following a set procedure to the letter. True prayer is surrender to the Lord in dialogue.

What is important is that prayer be a true expression and sharing of who we are, and that we be open to listening to what God has to say to us.

PRAYER. *May I always be ready to speak with You, Lord, and even more ready to listen to You.*

THE devil is afraid of us when we pray and make sacrifices.

—St. Anthony of Padua

DEC. 20

Defeating the Devil

REFLECTION. When one reads certain books or listens to certain people, one would almost think that the devil is just as powerful as God. That is not the case. Satan is only a creature.

The way Jesus defeated him was by dying on the Cross out of love for us. When we take up our crosses in prayer and sacrifice, Satan is once again defeated.

PRAYER. *May the love that I choose to live defeat the forces of evil and darkness.*

BE JOYFUL, seek the best, and let the sparrows chirp. —Pope St. John XXIII

DEC. 21

Who Cares What Others Say?

REFLECTION. When Pope St. John XXIII speaks of letting the sparrows chirp, he is saying that we should not be terribly concerned about what people say of us. Our self-worth should not be based upon others' opinions.

If they gossip, if they misjudge our motives, if they lie about us, it matters not—as long as we are doing the best that we can.

PRAYER. *Lord, let me find my peace in You alone.*

BE HUMBLE and patient, and the Lord Jesus will give you the will and the means.
—St. John Bosco

DEC. 22

We Are Not on Our Own

REFLECTION. When we are doing something, humility recognizes that we are not in charge and that we need God's help. Patience recognizes that things will come to fruition in God's time and not ours.

By being humble and patient, we allow God to do His part, and we show that we trust in His Providence.

PRAYER. *Lord, may I never be arrogant and impatient in what I am doing.*

IF YOU learn everything except Christ, you learn nothing. If you learn nothing except Christ, you learn everything.
—St. Bonaventure

DEC. 23

True Knowledge and True Wisdom

REFLECTION. St. John Kanty was a man of great learning in the areas of Sacred Scripture, theology, and physics. He also was an example of great charity toward the poor.

Yet, the thing that was most important in his life was his faith. This is evidenced by his pilgrimage to Jerusalem and his four pilgrimages (on foot) to Rome. The goal of his every journey was the Lord.

PRAYER. *May I always use my learning to serve others and for the praise of Your Name.*

CHRIST is the first-born of every creature, and the whole of humanity as well as the created world finds its foundation and meaning in Him.

—St. Lawrence of Brindisi

DEC. 24

Christ Is the Center of It All

REFLECTION. The day before Christmas is a wonderful time to remember how incredible it is that Jesus, the Son of God, embraced the humble call to be born as a child in Bethlehem.

Jesus took on our flesh so that we might share in His Divinity. All of creation is consecrated by His presence among us.

PRAYER. *O Christ, You are my Alpha and Omega. You are the source of all, and the goal toward which we proceed.*

YOU are beauty, you are gentleness.

—St. Francis of Assisi

DEC. 25

Words Fail

REFLECTION. How can we describe the wonder and glory of it all? When St. Francis spoke of the Birth of the Baby Jesus in Bethlehem, he licked his lips as if these were the sweetest words he had ever said.

We say prayers, we sing songs, but at a certain point words fail us—and we stand in awe before the mystery of God's love.

PRAYER. *Holy Infant, so tender and mild, sleep in heavenly peace.*

WE OUGHT to laugh and rejoice together with the Blessed Mary on the occasion of the Birth of her Son. —St. Anthony of Padua

DEC. 26

The Joy at the Birth of Jesus

REFLECTION. The birth of every child brings joy to this world, but how much more the Child Who is the Son of God!

In spite of the humble conditions into which the Child Jesus was born, and the danger the Holy Family was soon to face from the murderous plans of King Herod, Mary experienced a profound joy that first Christmas.

PRAYER. *May the joy of my Christmas be like Mary's joy, one that is pure and holy.*

FRANCIS loved Christ so fervently and Christ returned his love so intimately that he seemed to have his Savior before his eyes continually. —St. Bonaventure

DEC. 27

A Love That Binds

REFLECTION. Today is the Feast of St. John the Apostle. In Assisi there is a fresco called *Madonna of the Sunset* in which Our Lady asks the Child Jesus who loves Him more, St. John or St. Francis. The Child Jesus is pointing at St. Francis.

St. Francis' greatness as a Saint is based most of all on how much he loved Our Lord.

PRAYER. *May I learn from St. John and St. Francis how, day by day, to fall more in love with You.*

THE Word of God belongs not to him who hears or speaks it, but to him who does it. —Bl. Giles of Assisi

DEC. 28

The Holy Innocents

REFLECTION. The Holy Innocents in Bethlehem could not speak, for they were too young. They could not understand what was said around them, for that gift had not yet been given to them. Yet, in their quiet innocence, they gave witness to the plans of the Lord.

The shedding of their blood was a tragedy that led to a triumph of love.

PRAYER. *Lord, let me give a witness as profound as did these little children.*

O MARVELOUS humility! O astonishing poverty! The King of Angels, the Lord of heaven and earth, is laid in a manger. —St. Clare of Assisi

DEC. 29

What Incredible Humility

REFLECTION. When we look at the Christmas crib, we often are filled with a good, warm feeling. It is beautiful, it is precious. But, ultimately, it should be astounding.

The Son of God surrendered His Godliness to become a little child. He Who could create a universe became a helpless babe. He to Whom we turn for help now asks us to care for Him.

PRAYER. *O little Child of Bethlehem, may You be praised forever.*

O POVERTY! O humility! The Lord of all things is wrapped in swaddling clothes!

—St. Anthony of Padua

DEC. 30

Holy Infant So Tender and Mild

REFLECTION. In these days after Christmas, we have the opportunity to reflect upon the incredible fact that the Only Begotten Son of God was born as a baby in the poorest of circumstances. He did not grasp onto the prerogatives of His Divinity.

We, too, are called to surrender our privilege and riches, like He did, to truly live as children of our Heavenly Father.

PRAYER. *O come, let us adore Him.*

YOU are our protector, You are our guardian and defender.

—St. Francis of Assisi

DEC. 31

This Is Where Our Hope Lies

REFLECTION. On this last day of the year, we have an opportunity to reflect upon what has happened over this past year and to think about what we hope for in the coming year.

It is the Lord who got us through our difficulties, and He will continue to do so. It is He Who is the source of our accomplishments and the goal of our hopes.

PRAYER. *Thank You for what You have done for me in the past. Protect and guide me this coming year.*

The Canticle of the Creatures

MOST High, all-powerful, good Lord,

Yours are the praises, the glory, and the honor, and all blessing,
To You alone, Most High, do they belong,
and no human is worthy to mention Your Name.

Praised be You, my Lord, with all Your creatures,
especially Sir Brother Sun,
Who is the day and through whom You give us light.
And he is beautiful and radiant with great splendor;
and bears a likeness of You, Most High One.

Praised be You, my Lord, through Sister Moon and the stars,
in heaven You formed them clear and precious and beautiful.

Praised be You, my Lord, through Brother Wind,
and through the air, cloudy and serene, and every kind of weather,
through whom You give sustenance to Your creatures.

Praised be You, my Lord, through Sister Water,
who is very useful and humble and precious and chaste.

Praised be You, my Lord, through Brother Fire,
through whom You light the night,
and he is beautiful and playful and robust and strong.

Praised be You, my Lord, through our Sister Mother Earth,
who sustains and governs us,
and who produces various fruit with colored flowers and herbs.

Praised be You, my Lord, through those who give pardon for Your love,
and bear infirmity and tribulation.
Blessed are those who endure in peace
for by You, Most High, shall they be crowned.

Praised be You, my Lord, through our Sister Bodily Death,
from whom no one living can escape.
Woe to those who die in mortal sin.
Blessed are those whom death will find in Your most holy will,
for the second death shall do them no harm.

Praise and bless my Lord and give Him thanks
and serve Him with great humility.

ISBN 978-1-947070-83-7
90000
9 781947 070837